FEISTY

THE ACCIDENTAL BEGINNING

MEGUMI BEAR

Go Feisty Publishing

PO Box 562

Medina, WA, 98039

www.GoFeisty.com

Printed in the United States of America.

First Edition: July 2025; Revised Edition: September 2025

Published by Go Feisty Publishing, an imprint of Ijiriya USA. Ijiriya USA copyrights the Go Feisty name and logo.

This book may be purchased in bulk for business, educational, or promotional use. For more information, please contact your local bookseller or Go Feisty Publishing at info@gofeslty.com

ISBN: 979-8-9991632-0-2

Library of Congress Control Number: 2025914515

CONTENTS

Introduction

This is the story of how a Tokyo career woman accidentally crashed into international marriage, motherhood, and a whole new identity in America. This is not a tale of quiet assimilation—quite the opposite.

Get ready to laugh. Maybe cry. And definitely rethink everything you thought you knew about "Japanese wives."

I hope this book lifts your spirit—and lights a little fire.

Based on a True Story

Well... only a few people know for sure. The rest is up to your imagination.

Before You Dive In

This is the second edition—re-edited and slightly expanded from the first release in July 2025.

This book is designed *my* way. Punctuation? Spacing? Chapter breaks? Not textbook-perfect. But hey, this is my story—told in my style. So let go of the rules and enjoy the ride.

Truly yours,

Megumi Bear
Fall 2025
Let's Go Feisty!

Special Thanks

Title Calligraphy:

Sachi Tanimoto, *Issenkai Japanese Calligraphy Association*

The nicest person you could ever learn calligraphy from—and a fellow immigrant mama in Seattle.

My Family

To John, Milou, and Milay—

Thank you for giving me endless stories worth telling.

I couldn't have written this without you—

both literally and emotionally.

You're the reason I can stay true to myself.

Even as an uncontrollable beast of a mama and wife,

you've somehow stuck with me.

Thank you for your patience—

And please, keep letting me stay wild.

THE ACCIDENTAL BEGINNING

Megumi Bear

Hinoe-Uma Story

A *Hinoe-Uma*
—a Fire Horse Woman—
devours men.

That's the superstition
Japanese people believe.

And I—

I *am* a Fire Horse.

A six-foot-tall,

full-powered

Fire Horse.

I haven't devoured any man yet.

Not yet…

CHAPTER 1
A BOOZY MISTAKE: HOW IT ALL BEGAN

Marunouchi, Tokyo, circa 1989—

"All right, folks!—HERE WE GOOOO!!
GRRRRRAAAAH!!!! "

I grabbed a Kirin Lager—the big one, 633 ml—and stood tall, legs wide apart, overflowing with *kiai* (fighting spirit). I raised the bottle over my head like a trophy and grinned.

"She's gonna chug that whole thing?" said the art director.

"I think she's serious," whispered the senior copywriter.

"Is this her… talent?" someone from HR blinked.

Clap. Clap. Clap.

And just like that, the chant began.

"Ikki! Ikki! Ikki!" (chug! chug! chug!)

I tilted my head back, wrapped my lips around the neck of the bottle, and let the golden nectar pour straight into my soul.

Gulp. Gulp. Gulp. Gulp. Gulp. Gulp...

Jaws dropped. One executive choked on his *edamame*.

I didn't stop.

"What... is happening?" whispered the VP.

"Apparently, she's the new copywriter."

"We... hired this?" he said, staring at HR.

HR looked away, as if it were wildly above their pay grade.

Hi. I'm Megumi.

A six-foot-tall Japanese woman.

Yes, woman. And this was my first week at my dream job—Tokyo's top ad agency.

THE agency. The one every wide-eyed college graduate in Japan dreams of joining. After surviving countless interviews and tests, we were the chosen ones. And somehow, I slipped in.

And this? This was the new hire "talent show." A room full of polished gems. Everyone was good at something. Someone sang a ballad in some foreign language. Someone else danced like it was muscle memory from a past life.

I did the one thing I do better than anyone else: made a full-sized beer disappear in one go.

No magic. Just gravity and guts.

By the time I hit the bottom of the bottle, I let out a mighty:

"PUH-HAAAAAH!"

And then…

"GU-EEEHHH!"

It echoed through the open-concept office like a foghorn. Someone dropped their chopsticks. The head of Creative froze mid-sip—mouth agape, beer dribbling down his chin.

I casually unfastened my belt, exhaled, and stood there —victorious.

"She chugged the whole bottle?… and burped?" whispered the new account exec.

"So… we're working with this monster now?" he added.

Yep. That's how my career began.

A sleek office in the heart of Tokyo.

Our clients? Olympic sponsors. Global brands. Even politicians. We were the ones shaping the world—one glossy ad campaign at a time.

My poor manager had just come back from a commercial shoot in Hollywood featuring a major celebrity, only to be told he now had to mentor me. Lucky guy.

I loved my job.

My business card was a golden ticket—it got me into places, meetings, and all kinds of mischief. No door was closed. No celebrity off-limits.

I worked on beer campaigns—among others, wrote ad copy that made executives cry (occasionally for the right reasons), and drank on the company's dime—well, yen.

I became the Queen of After Five.

The office fridge was stocked with client-gifted booze. Technically, for researching. And I was the the most dedicated researcher on the team.

We worked nonstop. The lights never went off. Late nights meant "research." I was always "researching" the perfect buzz to come up with great copy.

And then one night, I got blackout drunk at the office. The blackout itself wasn't new. The phone call I made during it? That was.

I woke up the next morning with a killer hangover and a sticky note stuck to my forehead. It read:

"You called someone named John. He's coming to Tokyo this weekend. Good luck."

I blinked.

John? Who the hell was John?

And then it hit me.

Sort of.

There had been talk about some American guy—John-something.

Tall. Blonde. Teaching English up north.

A friend mentioned him once.

"You should date my friend John."

"Why?"

"He's taller than you."

"Okay, then I'll marry him."

I vaguely remember that conversation over tons of beer and sake at an *izakaya* one night.

I'm huge. I'm loud. And in Japan? That's not "cute." Or anywhere else, to be honest. Guys don't hit on me. I don't get second dates.

So I roar: "If he's taller than me, that's all I need! I'll marry him!"

And I mean it. That night, I think I really did.

Apparently, during my blackout, I used the office phone to call him. (Back when phones sat on desks and numbers hid in wallets.)

According to my sources, I screamed something like,

"Come see me in Tokyo, babyyyyy!"

—and passed out at my desk. I didn't remember getting home. Someone must've shoved me into a taxi. By then, they were practically trained professionals at dealing with my drunken exits.

So, who was this John?

Turns out, he was my classmate from a tiny college in the American Midwest. I spent two years there. He had never once caught my eye, so he probably wasn't my type. But for some reason (let's call it intensive late-night research), we were about to meet.

He took my call seriously.

He called back, and said, "See you Saturday!" Then he boarded the *Shinkansen*—Japan's bullet train (ridiculously on time)—Tokyo-bound and Megumi-magnetized.

I spotted him crouched by the famous panda statue in Ueno Station, reading *manga* (comic books from

Japan. Not just for kids. Sometimes not even safe for adults!), wearing a pair of oversized geeky glasses.

My first thought?

Oh no. I knew it. He's not hot.

I almost walked away.

Then he stood up.

My friend was right. He was tall. And I thought,

Huh. Maybe I'll give him the weekend.

I went up to him and said hi. I agreed to show him around Tokyo. Not because I liked him. Not because I wanted anything. Just because I told him to come. I'm a woman of my word. When sober, anyway.

"PUH-HAAAH!"

"GU-EEEHHH!"

Of course, we went to an *izakaya*. We found a "*nomi-hodai*"—all-you-can-drink. Japan's greatest gift to humanity.

"All-you-can-drink for two hours?" John gasped.

"Yep," I said, already three mugs deep.

"And you pay 3,000 yen, but I only pay 2,000 yen because I have a uterus."

"Wait. What?" he blinked.

"Ladies' Special. I am a lady, you know! Ladies get to drink cheap until even tequila starts to taste like water."

I wasn't trying to charm him. I wasn't pretending to be cute or delicate. I was just… me. All six feet of me.

And drink I did. Mug after mug of beer.

"PUH-HAAAAH!"

"GU-EEEHHH!"

My burp is a masterpiece.

A sonic boom of pride.

The waitress showed no signs of fear. She just kept the beers coming. I think she liked me. Maybe she burps like a beast too.

"So the rumors were true,"

John said, grinning.

"Huh?"

"In college, people said you could outdrink football players. I didn't believe it. Until now."

He knew.

He knew about me.

The Japanese girl at a tiny Midwestern college who played varsity basketball, drank with the football team, and wrecked linebackers like they were light beer. I beat them at Beer Bomb, every single time.

We'd never spoken before. But he remembered me.

So when he got a drunken call from the legendary Japanese girl he never had the guts to talk to, he thought:

"This must be fate."

And so, he came to Tokyo.

"Can't believe we're meeting like this, 7,000 miles from campus,"

he said, pouring me another beer.

"Cheers,"

I muttered, slightly impressed and deeply buzzed. He watched me drink like I was a fireworks show. Not judging. Just… delighted.

He was weird.

But the nice kind of weird—the kind that hands you tissues when you cry and holds your hair when you puke. He was the only one who didn't flinch at my size, my voice, my appetite, or my epic belching.

"Bigger is better,"

he said, refilling my mug.

"Even ramen's better when it's extra large," he added.

"And *gyoza*. And fried rice. Bonus points if they come free," I said.

"God made people in all shapes and sizes,"

he said, like some Zen monk.

"That's how it's supposed to be. Big means more room to love," he said.

I let out a burp that could wake the dead. He didn't even blink. Just poured more beer.

For the first time in 23 years, I forgot I had a height complex. Ever since kindergarten, I've always been a head taller than everyone else. Always towering. Always visible.

I learned early on—if I didn't want to be picked on, I had to be strong. So I got loud. I got fast. I got tough. Before anyone could laugh at me, I made them laugh with me.

At work, there were tall, good-looking guys too. Over six feet, sharp suits, perfect teeth—the kind of Japanese men who practically screamed "elite upbringing."

But tall guys liked tiny girls. I was just… too much. Too tall, too loud, too everything.

Then came this American guy—

I kept drinking, and he kept pouring.

By the end of the night, he asked:

"So… are we dating now?"

I squinted at him through my beer goggles.

"Are you out of your mind? You're tall, blond, blue-eyed. You could date anyone in Japan. Girls in the countryside would line up just to take photos with you."

He tilted his head.

"Yeah, I've noticed."

Then he smiled.

"But they're not you."

"You're clearly insane."

"Maybe. But I like what I like."

"I'm loud, big, and burp like a foghorn."

"Exactly."

"I'm a *Hinoe-Uma*, you know. Ever heard of that?"

"You mean the Zodiac thing that only comes around every 60 years?"

—Bingo.

I was born in 1966—the infamous Year of the *Hinoe-Uma,* the Fire Horse.

In Japan, that makes me legendary… in the worst way.

There's a delightful superstition: women born in that year are said to devour men. Not romantically.

Literally. Spiritually. Emotionally. Maybe physically, too.

The panic ran so deep, the birth rate nosedived in 1966. Japanese OB-GYNs panicked. Some even considered shutting down for the year.

And still, my parents went for it.

"Let's make a baby!"

Thanks, Mom and Dad. Bold choice.

I turned to him and said, "You sure you know what you're getting into? *Hinoe-Uma* women eat men alive."

He shrugged, "I'll do my best not to get eaten."

"I am strong-willed, you know."

"I like strong women."

I paused. The room spun slightly.

"… AND I drink like a fish."

"I've noticed," he said with a smile.

"I've got big feet, too."

He grinned.

"Even better. More to love."

"They're really stinky, too…"

I gave him every warning label possible, but he still wanted in. So we started dating. A two-hour *Shinkansen*, long-distance relationship.

I announced to the world that I finally had a boyfriend. My friends were ecstatic.

"Do NOT mess this up," said one.

"This guy deserves a medal. Or hazard pay."

"He's Gandhi," said another.

"You're the chaos. He's the calm."

My parents had already made peace with the idea of me dying alone in a Tokyo apartment surrounded by empty beer cans and expired *izakaya* discount coupons, and were stunned with joy.

"Bravo! I knew there would be some odd-taste man out there!!" my dad cheered.

"Get pregnant before he changes his mind!" my mom urged.

When my younger brother met him for the first time, he got down on his knees—full-on Japanese *dogeza* style—and pleaded:

"Please marry her. We're exhausted."

He must have been tired of picking me up from various sketchy night spots across Tokyo.

"And the sale is final. No returns accepted."

He added politely and seriously.

Apparently, the people in my life had reached full emergency consensus:

Marry. That. Man.

And honestly? I was starting to agree.

He pours beer. When I burp, he just nods like it's perfectly normal. He knows I am *Hinoe-uma,* and he does not care. He never asks me to shrink. He does not try to change me.

That's not just rare.

That's sacred.

"Fine," I thought.

What's the worst that could happen?

So I decided.

I'll marry him.

I was having a moment—like, *Wow, look at me, doing something normal and girly for once!*

And just then—

Right on cuc—

From across the Pacific Ocean—

A voice thundered:

"GRRRRRAAAAH!!!

WHAT THE HELL DO YOU THINK YOU ARE DOING?!"

No, it wasn't my ex.

It was his mother.

From California.

—And she was not happy.

She was ready for war.

CHAPTER 2
DEAREST FUTURE MOTHER-IN-LAW... FROM HELL

John sent an airmail to his parents.

A real letter. Ink on paper. Licked the stamp. International post. Good old-fashioned communication.

In his perfectly polite, painfully honest handwriting, he wrote: "I've decided to marry Megumi." Along with a photo of us.

His mother didn't just clutch her pearls. She ripped our photo in half like it was a cease-and-desist letter from her dreams and roared:

"WHAT THE HELL DO YOU THINK YOU ARE DOING?!"

"YOU THINK I'M GONNA LET MY SON GET KIDNAPPED BY A FOREIGN GIANTESS?!"

Suddenly, the wedding was not in the picture. It became an international hostage situation.

She had loaned her precious firstborn son to Japan on a two-year lease agreement—not donated him. And clearly, the lease had expired. But he hadn't come back!

She had heard rumors he was dating someone in Japan. But in her mind, you date abroad, you dump abroad. What happens in Vegas stays in Vegas.

Then—she went full Godzilla.

"DUMP THE GIRL IN JAPAN AND COME BACK TO AMERICA!"

Panicked, like someone trying to deprogram a cult victim.

Next thing we know—she's launching counterattacks via handwritten missiles. Each one wrapped in aggression and sprinkled with xenophobia.

First:

A VHS tape of the Pearl Harbor attack, with the handwritten message:

"REMEMBER PEARL HARBOR! JAPANESE DID THAT. REMEMBER!!"

Then:

Some god-awful B-grade *samurai* movie.

It featured *samurai* chopping off heads, blood spraying like busted ketchup packets, and dramatic slow-mo sword fights with questionable acting.

Message taped to the box:

"THIS is her heritage. WAKE UP! BEFORE IT'S TOO LATE!"

She was trying to scare him straight.

To her, I was a sneaky foreign woman stealing her precious American son. She genuinely believed she could change his mind with VHS horror and historical trauma.

And honestly? I was impressed. Where in California do you even find this stuff?!

Meanwhile, John just read her letters calmly, like weather forecasts.

"Hmm. Mom's not thrilled," he'd say, sipping his green tea.

I just sat there, stunned. Not because she hated me. But because she thought this drama would somehow make him unmarry me.

Lady, I'm not your enemy.

I'm your son's very tall, very thirsty destiny.

Now listen—if his mom had just said,

"Don't marry that alcoholic woman!"

I might've said,

"Fine enough. Maybe I should just marry booze instead."

And who knows—I might've bowed out gracefully, taken the hint, ended things then and there.

But no.

She didn't stop at "alcoholic." She went full-on racist villain with:

"DON'T MARRY THAT BARBARIC JAPANESE WOMAN!

YOUR FUTURE KIDS WILL TURN OUT TO BE CROSS-CULTURAL WACKADOODLES WITH NO IDENTITY!

Oh, wackadoodles? Really?

That's what we're doing now?

I'll pop out the wildest little half-Japanese wackadoodles you've ever seen!

This wasn't just about love anymore.

She wasn't just anti-*me*.

She was anti-my *entire culture*.

She was lumping all of Japan—all 120 million of us—into her ignorant little hate bubble.

How dare she?

Well, guess what, lady? Remember Nagasaki? Remember Hiroshima?

My father's house was bombed by American B-29s. He survived in a field of ashes.

My uncle fought in the war and never came back. There's no body in his grave—just his shoes.

And still, my family doesn't hate Americans!

My grandmother, who lost her beloved firstborn son in that war, once met John. I introduced him as "a friend from college." She smiled and said, in perfect textbook English:

> "May I help you? …This is all I know in
> English."

I almost cried.

She had learned that one phrase during the American occupation of Japan, to speak to the American soldiers who passed through her town after the war.

Even after all the destruction, she greeted them with kindness. With dignity. That's how she chose to respond.

That's how far we've come.

That's how much we've healed.

And then here comes this woman—John's mom— dragging history back like it's her emotional support trauma.

That was it.

I was done playing nice.

Fueled by love, sake, and righteous fury, I decided to dedicate my entire being to one goal:

DEFEAT THE RACIST.

Our love would be a symbol of global harmony.

This wasn't just a relationship.

This was me, sacrificing my young and fabulous body in the name of eternal justice.

One famous Japanese creative director once told me, upon hearing I was dating an American:

"Wonderful. As long as blood mixes, the world moves toward peace."

He took a long drag of his cigarette and looked off like a philosopher.

And you know what?

He was right.

So yes.

Let our blood mix.

Let this yellow-skinned, loud-laughing, beer-guzzling woman be accepted as your daughter-in-law, lady.

Watch me steal your son and launch world peace from my uterus.

And those terrifying half-Japanese, half-"whatever you call normal" grandkids you feared? Oh, they're coming. One after another. Cute, chaotic little hybrid bombs of multicultural joy.

I'm not just marrying your son.

I'm leading the charge for love, unity, and racial reconciliation. Move over, Gandhi. Step aside, Mother Teresa. I'm doing humanitarian work. With my whole body.

Time to show her what a real *Yamato Nadeshiko*—a traditional Japanese "perfect woman" prototype—is made of.

Not the quiet, tea-serving, "Yes, dear" kind.

No.

I am *Hinoe-Uma.*

I am the fire-breathing, headband-wearing, beer-chugging battle maiden version.

I never thought this "let's get married" thing would spiral into an international grudge match with an angry American mom.

But hey.

Life's full of surprises.

Now I was on fire.

Fueled by rage, patriotism, and leftover sake.

Japan never invaded the American mainland during World War II.

Fine. I'll do it myself—for love.

"John," I growled,

"We're going to America."

He blinked.

"Wait, I'm going too?"

"OF COURSE YOU ARE, YOU DINGBAT!"

He stood there like this was someone else's romantic war. Like I was dragging him into some mess.

Boy, please.

I marched us to the travel agency (yes, people still did that) and bought two plane tickets.

At the ad agency, we were all burning the candle at both ends. No sleep. No breaks. Paid leave? Technically yes. Take it? Get side-eyed into retirement. But I didn't care.

Steam blowing out of my nose, I stormed into my boss's office.

"I need time off," I said.

"To do what?"

"To FIGHT in AMERICA!"

He looked like he was trying to process it… and failed spectacularly. I walked straight to the Client Visit Board—the sacred calendar of meetings and outings—grabbed a marker, and wrote in bold, confident strokes:

AMERICA.

No details. Just **AMERICA.**

Coworkers stared. Then one of them—high from over-working—stood up and saluted.

"Do it for Japan!"

He cheered like I was an Olympic athlete. Don't worry. I'll bring home the gold.

This was the final showdown that World War II never delivered: a full-scale invasion of the American suburbs. And I was ready.

Up in the air—

"Brace yourself, woman!"

I crushed the tiny bottle of airplane whiskey in my hand.

And him? My fearless partner in this international romance?

Yeah. He was drooling in his sleep. Mouth open, head back, like a baby bird waiting for snacks.

"Wake up, fool!" I hissed.

"We're going into battle!"

"Wha—yes ma'am," he muttered, blinking.

Honestly, I couldn't wait to meet the woman who raised this floppy, sweet, clueless piece of man *tofu*.

The captain announced our final descent.

Below us: enemy territory.

Listen up, future Mother-in-Law.

You're wrong.

Dead wrong.

This was it.

The fuse was lit.

Operation: Mother-in-Law Showdown— Commence.

CHAPTER 3
JAPANESE INVASION OF THE AMERICAN SUBURBS

My future mother-in-law was very tiny.

Pocket-sized with a permanent frown and the energy of a suspicious owl. When I showed up at the airport, she had a full system crash.

This was not the Japanese woman she had pictured in her nightmares. I was bigger, louder, and clearly not here to ask for permission.

Yeah, lady. I can speak English. I out-earn your son. My shoe size is 27.5 centimeters. I'm the Japanese beast that came for your family tree!

But even though she was clearly terrified, I had to give it to her—she was tough.

"Hi Jo~hn! Welcome back, sweetie!" she squealed, throwing her arms around him like he was returning from war.

Kissy-kissy, clingy-clingy.

And me? The glorious *Yamato Nadeshiko* blooming proudly behind him?

Invisible.

She didn't even blink in my direction. I was literally looming over them like a benevolent Godzilla in heels, and this woman just acted like I wasn't even there.

I waved.

Nothing.

I shifted positions.

Nothing.

I even did a weird little hop-step thing to try and enter her field of vision.

Not even a blink.

"HELLO? I'M THE REASON YOUR SON'S BEEN MISSING FOR MORE THAN TWO YEARS!"

No response.

Finally, John stepped in—unable to watch the train-wreck unfold any longer.

"Mom, this is Megumi."

"Nice to meet you."

I gave her my biggest, brightest, most over-the-top smile.

And this woman?

She gave me the coldest, driest, most reluctant "Hello" ever squeezed through clenched dentures—

"Huh-lo."

That's it.

No eye contact. No handshake. No "welcome to the family" awkward hug. Nothing.

She turned her back on me, looped her arm around her darling son, and strutted off toward the car.

So, naturally, I did what any polite, culturally respectful Japanese woman would do in that moment:

I gave her the finger.

Full middle.

Right to the back of her over-orchestrated Beethoven-esque wig, she calls her hair.

In the car waiting for us was an older gentleman who looked exactly like Colonel Sanders—the KFC guy whose statue is plastered all over Japan, always smiling and greeting fried chicken lovers with unsettling cheerfulness.

This was John's dad. I secretly decided to call him Colonel Dad.

He'd been married to that pint-sized tyrant for over forty years.

A living legend. A tragic cautionary tale. Stone-faced. His expression said it all:

I've learned not to speak unless spoken to—or unless there's a tornado warning.

And so we drove.

In silence.

Toward the house where my future husband had grown up, and where my patience was about to go into retirement.

In the car, John's mother refused to talk about Japan. Not a word. Not a syllable. Not even a stray sushi reference.

Was this part of her deprogramming strategy? Like, if she pretended Japan didn't exist, maybe her son would forget he ever went there? And me? I'd just evaporate like leftover beer in the sun?

John's mother kept gushing about all of John's old friends I'd never heard of. Apparently, they were all wildly successful, rich, probably had excellent posture, and—shocking—not living in Japan.

"Don't you think it's time you came back and got a real job?" she cooed.

Good thing I never tried to impress her. I mean, thank heavens I didn't show up in a *kimono* with a tea whisk. I would've embarrassed myself straight into another century.

She just wanted her son back—minus me.

I, meanwhile, sat in the backseat like a cultural monument she refused to acknowledge.

I'm six feet tall—hard to miss. And yet—this woman managed to completely ignore my existence.

My parents, back in Japan, had very different attitudes.

"Don't lose this man!" they said.

"Humanity is one big family! Souvenirs will save the world!"

They loaded my suitcase like it was a mobile museum of Japanese culture: *kokeshi* dolls, *koi*-shaped windsocks, *origami* kits, fans, chopsticks, tea canisters, and lucky cats. A full-blown soft power campaign shoved between my socks.

John had once told me that his mom liked those Yoku Moku cookies—delicate butter and rich chocolate rolled into one dangerously addictive bite—and castella cake, the fluffy Nagasaki sponge cake with old Portuguese roots.

So my mom blasted off to Yokohama Takashimaya like it was a diplomatic emergency, bought an entire shelf's worth of Yoku Moku and top-tier castella, and declared:

"These will win her heart."

Spoiler: They did not.

When I offered these treasures to the Queen of Frost, she muttered a flat, dead-eyed "Thank you," and stacked the boxes like bricks on a side table in the corner of the living room.

I even tried to help.

"You'll want to eat the castella soon," I said sweetly.

"It's best fresh."

She didn't move.

Didn't even glance.

So there it sat—that beautiful, honey-gold castella, brought lovingly across the Pacific Ocean… gathering dust, growing mold, and quietly dying on the side table.

I threw another middle finger at her back.

CHAPTER 4
TYRANT AND THE CLAN

John grew up in Southern California.

He was the oldest of four siblings, raised in a perfectly average house with a killer location just steps from S University. Colonel Dad was a professor at the university—not a bad gene pool for our future "wackadoodles" to inherit.

And his mom?

Well… Let's just say she discovered the true American Dream—a woman's dream, really: outsource motherhood.

Thanks to the house's prime location, she hired university students—cheaply, of course—to babysit her four kids while she swanned around campus pretending to be some sort of academic goddess.

She never changed a single diaper. Not one.

The students did all the dirty work. And when they weren't around? Colonel Dad was on diaper duty. Yes, the professor. A physics professor, to be exact—now in charge of poop management.

This woman bossed around college kids and her own husband, skipped all the hard parts of parenting, and still walked around like she deserved a Nobel Prize in motherhood.

No chores. No diapers. No bedtime stories.

Just opinions. Lots and lots of opinions.

The kids?

Well, they grew up fast. From the moment they could walk, they learned to do everything on their own. Cook, clean, work part-time jobs, earn their own allowance—they practically raised themselves.

They barely saw their parents. The only thing more distant than their childhood memories… was their actual mother.

This woman skipped the hard part of child-rearing and then—when her kids finally grew up and tried to live their own lives—she clamped down like a villain in a Disney sequel.

"YOU WILL LIVE THE LIFE

I IMAGINED FOR YOU!"

Did any of her four kids stand up to her?

Nope.

Not one.

Family bonding time—

There I was, trying to blend in like a humble little outsider, sitting quietly at the far end of the dinner table like someone being judged in a silent contest she never entered.

The Grand Matriarch was running her nightly roll call. One by one, she asked everyone what they'd like to do tomorrow.

"John?"

"Whatever's fine." (Classic John. No opinions, just vibes.)

"Bill?"

"How about a movie?"

"Mary?"

"I'd love to go bowling."

"Ed?"

"Yeah, I vote for a movie too."

And then—

… My turn never came.

She just stood up and declared,

"Well, that settles it. A movie it is!"

Later, I overheard her chatting with a neighbor.

"I heard John's fiancée from Japan is visiting?"

And she snapped:

"Oh no, she's just a friend."

JUST A FRIEND?!

My fists shook with pure fury.

Then one night, a miracle: John offered to treat the whole family to dinner. He even picked the restaurant —his favorite little Italian place down the street.

"Yeah! That's my man! Feast tonight!"

We arrived.

We waited.

And then…

The Tiny Tyrant vanished.

"Where'd she go?" I whispered.

"Bathroom," someone said.

"Probably yelling at the plumbing," I muttered.

But when she returned, she was smiling.

Smiling.

Which meant danger. She clapped her hands and chirped:

"Well, this place is too noisy, so I called another restaurant and made a new reservation. Let's go!"

SHE HAD USED THE BATHROOM BREAK TO MAKE A COUNTER-RESERVATION.

From a payphone.

Yes, kids. It was the pre-cellphone era, and evil still found a way.

This was John's night! His treat. His favorite restaurant. This was his one moment to be a man of action! So naturally, I cheered him on:

"Stand up to her! Come on! This is YOUR dinner!"

And John said:

"…We can't. My mom's always right. We… we don't go against her."

I grabbed his arm.

"Are you serious? We're already here. Just stay!"

But no.

He peeled away and followed her out the door.

I couldn't believe what I was seeing. I grew up arguing with my parents like it was a family tradition. Why didn't anyone say:

"Hey! John's the one paying—sit down and hush!"

Or:

"You can't just hijack dinner plans like this!"

But no.

No one said anything.

They all climbed into the car.

Silently.

Nobody resisted.

They just… obeyed.

IS THIS NORMAL?!

Do American mothers really hold this much power?

Is that… legal?!

At that moment, I realized—this wasn't about me marrying into the family.

This was a rescue mission.

I had to liberate this poor, brainwashed clan from their tyrant queen. I had to show her the truth:

The world does not bend to your will, lady.

NOT ANYMORE.

All right then.

Lady Liberty, reporting for duty.

Torch in one hand, rage in the other.

I wasn't just going to marry into this family—I was here to liberate it. They needed a full-blown regime change.

I was the fresh gust of revolutionary wind they never asked for but desperately needed.

I would bring freedom.

I would bring justice.

I would bring… attitude.

With my nostrils flared and my mission locked in, I began shadowing John like a giant uninvited plus one at all times.

Whenever The Mother wanted to talk to her dearest firstborn, I'd be right behind him, looming like an emotional security system. Six feet tall, silent, and slightly terrifying. The Mother would say something like,

"Today, you should go chop firewood in the mountains."

And I'd whisper to John in Japanese:

"ババアに川に洗濯に行くと言え。(Tell her you're going to the river to do laundry.)"

John became a puppet, and I became the belly-speaking puppet master of polite rebellion.

For the first time in his life, John started saying no to his mother. Not because he'd grown a spine, but because I was standing directly behind him, and his mother feared me more than losing control.

Eventually, John started enjoying it. Tasting the sweet forbidden fruit of… disobedience.

Little by little, our gentle puppet evolved.

And one glorious day, he finally declared, with the confidence of a man possessed:

"If you don't let us get married, then... *ENGA-CHO!*"

Yes. He actually said *ENGA-CHO.*

A childhood curse word used by Japanese kids that loosely translates to:

"You're cursed with cooties forever."

He was back.

Rewired. Rebooted. Reintegrated into society as a free-thinking human being.

I stood behind him, arms crossed, chin up, glowing like the Statue of Liberty at sundown.

"ENGA-CHO?!"

That shook her.

The Mother—who once disowned her entire family for love (and for Colonel Dad)—was now about to get the same treatment from her son.

No... not my sweet baby boy... Don't cast me aside! I changed your diapers—well, technically, the students did, but still!

But still… a Japanese daughter-in-law?

Her prim little spine quivered.

She prayed.

"Oh Lord… Buddha… any benevolent higher being…or even just some random blonde floozy with blue eyes—PLEASE, someone seduce my son!"

"ANYONE BUT THE GIANT JAPANESE WOMAN!"

But deep down, she knew. She didn't have the charm or the budget to pull off a counter-romance campaign. Even if she threw a mountain of cash at the problem, it's not like a parade of American Barbies were lining up at the door saying,

"Ooooh, I must have him."

Nope. There was no better candidate than me.

I mean, sure—I'm a little loud. And tall. And possibly terrifying in the right lighting.

But I committed.

I looked past his questionable wardrobe and mild social paralysis and saw the potential inside. I had a fondness for this *tofu* floppy man.

"Yes, I'll take this man and raise him into something resembling a functioning adult."

You're welcome.

Meanwhile, she paced. Her Beethoven-esque wig was bouncing like it had its own opinions. Her hands were clutching her temples like she was auditioning for a tragic opera.

"What... am I going to do with this?"

She had lost control. The Reign of Terror was crumbling.

And somewhere in the distance, the Statue of Liberty (me) raised her imaginary sake cup and whispered:

"Game on!"

CHAPTER 5
A FAREWELL ACROSS
THE PACIFIC

"Um… m… may I speak to Megumi…
please?"

Midway through my Great American Invasion Tour,
the phone rang.

It was from Japan—my younger brother. Yes, THE
brother. The one who had once dropped to his knees
and begged John to marry me.

He speaks English just fine, but apparently not enough
to be comfortable talking to *her*.

The Mother had answered the phone and passed it to
me like it was something suspicious. Possibly
contagious.

I figured my family just wanted an update. A status
report from the front lines. So I took the phone with
swagger and said:

"Victory is ours!"

Like some overconfident general broadcasting from occupied territory.

But instead of laughter—or a classic sibling snark attack—my brother spoke quietly.

"Grandma has passed away."

Just like that, I was on a plane heading home alone.

Back across the Pacific.

Back to say goodbye.

Remember my grandma?

She had smiled at John and said, in her only English phrase:

"May I help you?"

That was it.

And that was everything.

This woman had lost her son to war. Lost her home. Lived in poverty.

And still smiled at the American boy I brought home.

My grandma was the best of humanity.

Why now?

Why when I wasn't there to be with her?

—Maybe she didn't want me to see her go.

Maybe she wanted my last memory of her to be smiling and strong.

Maybe she knew I had found someone I loved, and thought I'd be okay.

They said that at the hospital, she turned to the nurse and whispered,

"Thank you. They've come for me."

And then, sometime later… she was gone.

Maybe her son—the one she lost in the war—came to take her home.

I flew back to Japan in tears.

I stood at her funeral in silence.

She—of all people—had no bitterness.

No hate. No grudges.

What would she have thought, knowing I was being rejected, just for being Japanese?

Would she have felt sad?

Angry?

While she was taking her final breath, I was across the ocean, being told I wasn't good enough. That I was wrong—just for being who I am.

This couldn't be the end of the story.

Not like this.

For her—for the woman who loved everyone without judgment—I had to prove it was possible. That a Japanese woman and an American man could fall in love and build a beautiful life.

My grandma wanted to see me in a wedding dress.

She dreamed of holding my child in her arms.

It'll all happen, Grandma.

You'll just have to watch from above.

I'm going to marry this man.

No matter what.

So listen up, Soon-to-be Mother-in-Law.

You can scowl.

You can ignore me.

You can pretend I don't exist.

But you can't stop this.

CHAPTER 6
YOUR SON IS A HOSTAGE

Lunch time in Morioka, Iwate—

"Uuuuughhh…"

"I can't do it anymore!"

One by one, the men dropped like flies. Meanwhile, I slammed down another empty bowl.

"More! Bring it on!!"

My nose was sweating, ears ringing, and I could practically feel *soba* noodles trying to exit through my pores. But I kept stacking those bowls with the rhythm of a factory robot fueled by ego and carbs.

Thank God I'm huge.

Sure, I drink like a camel on vacation, but my stomach? Straight-up hippopotamus class.

This was Morioka—an old castle town up in northern

Japan, proud home of extreme *soba*-eating. And this was the legendary *Wanko Soba* challenge.

If you've never heard of it, *Wanko Soba* isn't a food. It's a sport. At least in my opinion.

You sit down, and a staff member starts dropping bite-sized bowls of *soba* in front of you. One after another. Relentless. No time to breathe.

You eat until you surrender by slamming a lid on your bowl. Until then? No mercy. No breaks. Just *soba*.

It's Japan's version of a hot dog-eating contest—but with slightly more dignity… usually.

Except today, I had none.

We were on location for a commercial shoot, with over twenty crew members—lighting guys, carpenters, set designers, videographers—all big, burly men who looked like they could wrestle bears and flip trucks before lunch. And I was the one who proposed the challenge:

"Let's do a *Wanko Soba* Eating Contest!"

Since no one in production dares say "no" to the client's agency, everyone just smiled politely and followed me straight into a noodle-fueled battlefield.

Why did I suggest it?

Because I needed the money.

Entry fee? 1,000 yen per person.

Winner takes all.

20 people × 1,000 yen = 20,000 yen.

I needed that 20,000 yen.

Desperately.

Me. The only woman in the group. With the most bowls stacked. Sweating *soba.* Eyes locked on the prize.

Working in advertising paid well—but I had a very expensive accessory.

A fiancé.

Or more accurately: a foreign freeloader.

John—formerly an English teacher in northern Japan —had moved to Tokyo to live with me and enrolled in a one-year Japanese language program.

A noble endeavor. Adorable, even. But let's be real: Tuition? Rent? Bento budget?

ALL ON ME.

This tender young salarywoman was funding the whole international romance operation.

If I didn't take care of him, he might listen to The Mother—still mourning the potential loss of her all-American family legacy—and head back to America.

And if that happened, she'd win.

And I would be the tragic loser in my own love story.

Nope.

Not happening.

I had to win.

And that meant winning my self-declared *Wanko Soba* Eating Contest. I ate like my life depended on it. Because it did.

Judge me all you want, Japan. Y'all weren't lining up to date me! So now I'm broke, living with a foreign guy who proudly holds a student ID, and zero income.

"I NEED THAT MONEY!! RAAAAAAAAWR-RRRRRRRRR—!!"

"Ughh… I give up…"

Finally, just as the button on my pants was about to launch across the room like a deadly missile, the last man gave up.

"YESSSS!"

Victory.

I tucked the precious cash into my wallet like it was emergency oxygen, then turned to the producer and said:

"So… how about a *Yakiniku* Eating Contest tonight?"

Tokyo was a peaceful place.

You know why?

No sign of The Mother.

The woman had one fatal weakness: She was terrified of airplanes.

"A giant metal object in the sky? That's unnatural!"

She said it like she was born in the Edo period.

So thankfully, The Mother couldn't just show up unannounced and kidnap her son back to America. She'd never survive a tanker ship either.

Which meant—Tokyo was safe. Quiet. Just us. Hallelujah.

—It's just that we were broke…

My female colleagues were out golfing with guys who drove BMWs and Mercedes, sipping wine in Michelin-starred French restaurants, living their best Tokyo lives.

Me?

I was replanting the stub of a green onion in a yogurt cup, hoping it would grow enough to be the only ingredient in miso soup.

I started looking forward to bento boxes handed out at commercial shoots. While everyone else groaned, "Bento again!" I was over there stuffing my face like I'd discovered foie gras. And when there were leftovers? I packed them up—zero shame—and brought them home to feed my personal foreign rescue project.

Still, the money always ran out. I even got creative—whenever we went out in a big group, I'd volunteer to pay with my credit card, collect cash from everyone, and use it to survive another week. Classic broke-girl maneuver. Desperate times, desperate measures.

My coworkers weren't shy about their opinions.

> "You're insane for spoiling that foreign guy."

> "He's bleeding you dry."

> "You're not dating—you're sponsoring."

And I'd snap back:

> "He's a hostage."

> "I'm keeping him from going back to the enemy."

> "This is about justice. This is about world peace!"

At which point, someone would gently pat my shoulder and say:

> "Okay, easy now. You need sleep. Or a therapist."

Everyone assumed I was broke and broken. Maybe I was—but I wasn't giving up.

I never expected a man to support me. That was never the plan. I was the breadwinner—and proud of it.

We lived in a tiny apartment.

And we had one *futon*. Just one. So we tacked on a *zabuton* (a flat cushion people sit on) to make it wider on the *tatami* floor.

I snored like a chainsaw and tossed like a boat in a storm.

John?

He always ended up smashed against the sliding *fusuma* door by morning. *Fusuma* doors are basically just fancy paper over wood. Not exactly sweat-proof.

Eventually, the lower half turned a mysterious yellowish shade—a perfect, life-sized sweat shadow of John. It was both romantic… and horrifying.

Now, here's the thing: In Japan, foreign guys—especially blond, white ones—are hot property. If you're even remotely good-looking, you can model, act, appear on TV—basically monetize your foreign-ness.

Back then, TV was filled with quirky foreigners who spoke fluent Japanese and got paid really well for it.

So I'd look at John and say:

"If only you had some talent, I could pitch you to an agency."

And he'd respond,

   "I can light my farts on fire."

Then flop on his back, legs in the air.

Poof.

A brief flicker of flame from his personal exhaust pipe.

… Sir.

Even the Little Match Girl saw roast turkey and warm fireplaces.

All I got was… a stinky smoke bomb.

Naturally, he showed off this "talent" to friends. Soon, he earned the nickname: *Onara* Boo (Fart Boo).

That's right. The man I was going to marry was now known as *Onara* Boo.

He existed in a different realm. A realm where trends, shame, and general public awareness did not exist.

Other than farting, his only real skill was… speaking English. Which, in Japan, was a prized currency.

Everyone wanted to speak English. There were English schools on every corner. So I sent him off to teach part-time, racking up just enough pocket change to keep us afloat.

Meanwhile, I hustled hard. I went around my ad agency selling him like a discount foreign voice actor.

"Need a narrator for your commercial? I've got a guy —only 10,000 yen! Total bargain!"

Normally, those slick-voiced foreigners who go "Hmm… Mandom" or whisper "Nescafé" at the end of ads get paid over a million yen for one line.

1,000,000 yen!

John? One line, 10,000 yen.

Fire sale pricing. Literal fire, if he got too excited.

Thanks to my guerrilla marketing, he landed a few gigs —TV extras, radio voiceovers—just enough to justify his existence.

In our crumbling Tokyo apartment, thick airmail envelopes from The Mother kept arriving.

Inside?

Graduate school applications. Business school forms. Full-blown Return-to-America propaganda packets.

You see, his one-year Japanese language program was almost over. We were just scraping by, surviving day to day.

But SHE?

She was already executing Operation Bring My Baby Home.

"You've learned Japanese—great! Now come back, get your MBA, and you can do anything here in America!"

She practically drooled over the thought of turning him into a bilingual trophy boy.

Well, guess what.

NO.

I didn't sacrifice my financial dignity so he could be vacuumed back into that woman's apron.

He's staying.

With me.

But right as I was burning with righteous fury, I glanced over… And there he was. Sharpening a pencil. Getting ready to study for the GRE or GMAT or whatever his mom told him to do.

ARE YOU KIDDING ME?

"IDIOT! Degrees are for cowards! You don't need more school—you need a job! Experience! That's what you lack! Get hired! Get Rich! Become one of those 'high-end foreign men' that get handed penthouses in Azabu!"

Sure, his mom was scary. But unfortunately for him, the woman he promised to marry was even more terrifying.

So John, thoroughly spooked, bought a big corporate directory and started cold-calling companies.

Page one.

First number.

"Hello… Do you want to hire an American?"

… Click.

That went well.

No one talked to him.

Receptionists laughed. Not once did anyone transfer his call past the front desk. It was less a job hunt and more a prank call marathon.

Eventually, having struck out with Japan Inc., he somehow stumbled upon a tiny, unknown foreign company in Okubo, Shinjuku.

He called.

"Hello… Do you want to hire an American?"

And someone said:

"YES! YES! COME IN RIGHT NOW!"

Wait, what? Really?!

"A company in Okubo?" I said.

"Sounds shady. Could be a scam. Or one of those sketchy back-alley joints. But whatever, think of it as practice. Go!"

I mapped out the train transfers for him, sent him off like a nervous puppy to possibly the sketchiest corner of Tokyo.

A few hours later…

He got the job.

Immediately.

I didn't know what the company did.

John said they were a "software" company.

What was software? Seriously—it was that era.

"Software?"

"Underwear company?"

"Porn studio?"

John explained to me, but I had no idea. But options were limited. So I said:

"Whatever. Just work. Earn. Stay in Japan."

He wasn't just a broke student anymore.

He had a job.

A salary.

A real paycheck.

Thank you, mysterious possibly-not-an-adult-video software company! You saved him from being deported by his own mother.

And thanks to you, we could finally afford meat again!

Victory never tasted so juicy.

CHAPTER 7
THE INVITATION

"Hello, Megumi. How are you? So… is John there?"

Another day, another transpacific sneak attack.

It was Colonel Dad—a solemn, chicken-less version of Colonel Sanders.

I could hear the woman's breathing in the background. Yes, HER. The Mother. The Tiny Tyrant. My future mother-in-law!

If she wanted to speak to her son so badly, why didn't she just call herself?

Oh, right.

Because she didn't want to accidentally speak to me. Heaven forbid. So she used Colonel husband as a human telephone stand. Every. Single. Time.

I always answered first.

Always.

She knew it—and she hated it. So once again, I smiled sweetly and said,

"Sure, he's here. One sec."

Then handed the receiver to John like it was a live grenade.

"Hi Mom!" he chirped.

Boom. She snatched the phone out of her poor husband's hand.

The war for her son's soul had been dragging on for over a year. What she once saw as a harmless cultural detour had now escalated into a full-blown international custody battle.

And unfortunately for her, the "hostage" she'd tried to rescue?

He got a job.

In Tokyo.

And wasn't coming back.

She was losing—and she knew it. So she escalated.

Her attacks kept coming.

Postcards from their hometown sealed in envelopes so I wouldn't see them.

Catalogs, flyers, junk mail—all forwarded to Tokyo like it was a battleground for his allegiance. Job ads from companies "looking for bilingual Americans." Nostalgic bait like,

"Remember little Jenny from elementary school? She's all grown up and back in town!"

And of course:

"There's a class reunion coming up—you could be back just in time…"

Translation?

"COME HOME. YOU BELONG HERE. NOT WITH HER."

The war had dragged on long enough.

Time for a decision, lady.

Get disowned by your beloved firstborn? Or raise the white flag… and accept me—the Giant Japanese Bride?

I leaned in. Pressed my ear against the other side of the receiver. Today, she was rambling on again:

"It's sunny here in California!"

"The job market is amazing!"

"Now's the perfect time to come home!"

Yeah, yeah. But not one word about me. She still believed this was reversible.

But oh, dearest future mother-in-law… can't you hear it? The wedding march was getting louder.

"Tell her to give you a clear answer about the wedding."

I whispered into John's ear like an angel of justice. Or a very tall, very intimidating voice of doom.

"Uh, Mom, about our marriage…"

he stammered.

There he was—caught between two demons, one on each side of the Pacific.

On one end of the line: The Mother, armed with guilt and emotional weapons of mass destruction.

On the other end of the *tatami* room: Me, serving death glares and heavy-duty relationship ultimatums.

John had never feared for his life quite like this. Poor guy was being emotionally waterboarded by two women who loved him in completely incompatible ways.

Only the Colonel—dear, checked-out, unbothered Colonel Dad—sat somewhere in the background like a decorative houseplant, spiritually detached from worldly drama.

Sensing defeat, the enemy finally sent in a compromise.

> "My mother would like us to come and travel together in California."

John relayed the message, eyes flicking nervously across my face.

Ohhh? So now the future mother-in-law wants *quality time* with me?

Cute.

Bring it on.

I was more than ready to let her soak in every glorious inch of this full-powered Japanese fiancée.

"Tell her I accept," I said.

Operation Final Battle: California, *initiated.*

With steam blowing out of my nose, I stormed into my boss's office—again.

"I need time off," I said.

"Again?"

"Again! Final boss fight. No time for presentations."

"Uh… okay. Good luck, I guess?"

I shoved my ad agency duties onto my slightly stunned boss, filed for time off, and we were off—straight into enemy territory.

It was the summer the bubble economy started to fizzle. But I had no time for economic trends.

I had a future mother-in-law to defeat.

CHAPTER 8
OPERATION FINAL BATTLE: CALIFORNIA

"Jooohn! Welcome *hoooome!*"

Smooch. Squeeze. Gush.

The Mother nearly tackled her precious firstborn with a combination of sloppy kisses and crushing hugs.

Me?

She threw me a flat "Hi."

No eye contact. No handshake. Definitely no hug. Zero growth, same old Queen Frostbite.

Fine.

Let the games begin. I wasn't here for her affection—I was here for the win.

So began the Grand 4-Night, 5-Day "Welcome to California" Tour.

The plan?

Four humans.

One car.

No escape.

Cast: Colonel Dad, The Mother, John, and me.

Destination: All over the damn state of California.

Sleeping arrangements? Motel rooms with connecting doors, or worse—couches.

This wasn't a vacation. This was a full-scale inspection. I was essentially under house arrest on wheels.

Every move I made was monitored, interrogated, and mentally scored by The Supreme Commander of the Anti-Megumi Task Force.

—And at the end of the trip? The Supreme Commander would hand down her ruling. No appeals. No mercy.

Of course, her itinerary was bananas.

Each motel was in a totally different direction. She desperately needed Google Maps—but it didn't exist yet. We relied on old-school AAA paper maps instead. She clearly didn't understand the scale of California.

Madness. Zero efficiency. Negative logic.

And yet—no good food. No local specialties. No drinks to numb the pain.

We drove all day until our butts went numb, only to

arrive at our destination at midnight, hungry and grumpy.

Every meal was a sad roadside diner pit stop.

Every bathroom break? Timed perfectly around The Mother's bladder.

And the car stereo? Nonstop gloomy classical music. Not the elegant kind, either—the funeral-slow kind.

—Dear Colonel Dad, please don't fall asleep at the wheel.

And then there was the daily interrogation.

This was psychological warfare. Planned by The Supreme Commander of of the Anti-Megumi Task Force.

Clearly, her goal was to break me—make me snap, make me flee.

But she underestimated who she was dealing with. I'm the granddaughter of a woman who lived through two wars, lost everything, and still raised a family with nothing but grit.

You really think I'm gonna give up now?

Think again, Queen of Doom.

Her interrogation ranged from politics to economics to "general knowledge" (read: obscure trivia designed to humiliate).

Sure, she couldn't fry an egg or change a diaper for any of her four kids, but she did have two advanced degrees she collected (and never used) while ignoring her kids.

Basically, this was harder and nastier than the ad agency entrance exam I bulldozed through with sheer physical stamina.

Picture this: I finally get out of the car. We're at a dusty diner. I open my mouth, ready to bite into a long-awaited hamburger—

The Mother, like a CIA operative disguised as a lunch companion, pounces.

"What are the three major inventions of the Renaissance?"

—Correct answer: gunpowder, the compass, the printing press. *Who the hell memorizes that?*

"If I wanted to sell Native American jewelry in Tokyo, what kind of marketing strategy would you propose?"

—Correct answer: *Lady, no one in Japan wants your cursed trinkets—stay home.*

Even the brief silences were booby-trapped. I pick up a fork, raise it to my mouth—and she strikes

"In our family, we use proper manners. Fork in the left hand, knife in the right. Isn't that right, John dear?"

Oh please.

I come from a nation where we handle *natto* and grilled fish with chopsticks—one hand, no mess, no drama. You people need two utensils just to wrangle a meatball. Don't talk to me about table manners.

I smiled through gritted teeth while cursing her in Japanese. And just when I finally leaned into my meatball pasta—fork obediently in my left hand, just like she wanted—

"Don't you care that John's put on weight?"

Excuse me?!

What kind of twisted logic is that? Now his weight is my fault?

When she finally got up to use the bathroom, I turned to John and socked him in the arm.

"It's your fat ass. YOU deal with her."

The woman attacked from every direction.

Even while she was on the toilet.

At a grimy highway rest stop bathroom, I tried to claim just a tiny moment of peace, perched on a questionable porcelain seat.

But nope.

Even here, I couldn't relax.

American public restrooms have that ridiculous 50-centimeter gap at the bottom of the stall doors. What if she crouched down and peeked in?

My bladder clenched up. My usually enthusiastic bowels got shy. Nothing was moving. Terror constipation.

The sky was blue, and birds chirped.

Mount Shasta stood tall and majestic in the distance.

But thanks to The Itinerary Tyrant's inhumane road-trip schedule, we had zero time to enjoy the scenery.

So I turned toward the great Mount Shasta and screamed in Japanese:

"やってられねえよ、ばかやろー!"

The Tyrant asked John,

"What's she barking about now?"

John calmly translated,

"She says she's grateful for the lovely weather."

(what I *actually* said: "**Screw this! You moron!**)

We had to coordinate bathroom breaks carefully, lest I end up peeing next to her. No, thank you.

If I dashed off alone, she'd seize the chance to grab John and hiss in his face—like a snake on a mission.

"If you're going to wake up, now's the time."

"Do you really want to marry internationally?"

"Whatever happened to that busty girlfriend from college?"

She still hoped he'd "come to his senses." That is, dump me and come crawling home.

The road trip from hell continued.

Out the window: Lake Tahoe.

Happy, tanned couples sailing by, holding hands like they'd just won a casting call for a toothpaste commercial.

Everywhere—white.

Was I delusional enough to think I could just... blend in?

The interrogation never ended.

Over the hills, through the woods, over psychological cliffs we *goooo~*

Why the hell did I blow all that money flying to America… just to get psychologically waterboarded?

I could've gone to Italy—eaten pasta, guzzled wine, and passed out like a happy Roman. Or gone to Spain and ridden a damn bull.

But no.

Here I was—being force-fed depressing diner food while enduring The Tyrant's full-blown Homeland Security interrogation.

I finally understood how torture makes people confess to crimes they didn't commit.

> Grandma, I'm sorry. I don't think I can get married after all. I just… I can't do this anymore.

Later, I told John:

"You know what? I don't care anymore. I'm done. We don't have to get married."

At the end of that long, soul-sucking day, I chugged the emergency bourbon I'd been hiding and collapsed like a dying cow.

Body broken.

Spirit crushed.

Let it go, I told myself.

I passed out—drunk, on a cheap mattress—finally able to sleep.

The last morning of our five-day hostage tour—we left the motel.

Another ten hours of driving loomed ahead.

But I didn't give a damn anymore.

Come on, Final Boss.

Hit me with whatever else you've got.

Say something offensive.

Ask me anything.

Do it.

I dare you.

Just feed me something decent.

Pour me a drink.

And let's get this over with.

I sat in the backseat—silent, seething, and, visibly annoyed.

That's when the Final Boss, riding shotgun, slowly turned to us and said:

"IF YOU'RE GOING TO GET MARRIED, DO IT NEXT SUMMER.

AT THE S UNIVERSITY CHAPEL.

I'VE ALREADY MADE THE RESERVATION."

CHAPTER 9
VICTORY...OR SO I THOUGHT

As legend has it, the night I passed out snoring from too much bourbon, John snuck off for a secret consultation with Colonel Dad.

And for once, the man—normally a wax statue permanently fused to his recliner—spoke.

He actually turned to his wife and said:

"John loves Megumi.

Not allowing this marriage is unacceptable."

Boom.

The wife, stunned that her silent husband had found his voice (and maybe remembering why she married him in the first place), paused. Softened.

And just like that, she cracked.

Victory.

The future mother-in-law was about to become the official mother-in-law.

She waved the white flag.

Was there a teary reconciliation? A heartfelt hug? A "Oh Mom, I'm so glad we're finally family!" moment?

Absolutely not.

Instead, the moment she surrendered, she evolved into The Wedding Dictator General.

Everything about the wedding?

Decided by her.

The date? August 29.

The venue? S University Chapel.

The officiant? Her pick.

Reception, catering, flowers, cake—even our honeymoon? All hers.

All I ever wanted was her blessing. Not the entire wedding under full authoritarian control.

Our Wedding Day—

The chapel was massive. Grand. Historic.

A local landmark—the kind that shows up on postcards. It could seat over a thousand people.

And somehow, she got it.

She probably booted some poor couple off the calendar just to lock in her dream wedding date.

There I was, standing at the chapel entrance, gripping my nervous dad's arm, staring down an endless aisle.

—Fifty meters of emptiness.

Only about twenty people had shown up, all clustered in the front row.

Most of them were mine—my parents, my siblings, the boss who'd watched over me like a guardian angel and even used his precious vacation time to be there for us from Japan, my host family from my exchange student days, and a few brave friends who dared to cross cultural lines for love.

John's side?

Just the immediate family. Not a friend. Not a cousin.

Time for the dramatic virgin aisle walk—

I turned to my dad.

> "Let's jog down this aisle, Dad."
>
> "Can't. My new shoes are giving me blisters."
>
> "Blisters?! You had one job! You knew this day was coming!"
>
> "Sorry, I'll break them in next time."

"Next time?!"

And so, like two sad penguins with bad knees, we waddled slowly down the world's longest, emptiest aisle.

If we were in Japan, the chapel would be packed with friends and coworkers—and I'd feel like a superstar bride...

Tears welled up.

I had dreamed of that dramatic, glamorous walk. Instead, it felt like a dress rehearsal for someone else's wedding.

—And then came the honeymoon horror.

That's right.

Our honeymoon.

With our parents.

"It's such a rare chance to all be together,"

said the now-official mother-in-law sweetly.

"We should all go!"

SIX of us.

Honeymooning.

Together.

I was now officially part of a family where freedom of speech did not exist.

The destination? Yosemite.

The hotel? The fanciest in the park—The Ahwahnee Hotel. Disney stayed there. JFK stayed there. Chaplin. The Queen of England. And yes, she booked the same suite the Queen once stayed in.

"Perfect for a honeymoon," she beamed.

For one hot second, I actually thought—Wow... maybe she's trying to do something nice.

Idiot.

The suite was stunning.

Huge. 2 bedrooms.

Bedroom 1: The Mother and Colonel Dad.

Bedroom 2: My parents.

Us?

She pointed to the couch in the living room.

This? For newlyweds?

No walls. No privacy. No romance. Just… couch.

The celebratory champagne meant for the newlyweds? She tried to take it home with her.

"This isn't a honeymoon—it's a trap! Who IS your crazy mother!?"

To which John, grinning and replied,

"Well... she's your mother now, too."

The war was over.

More than two years of combat, and John finally chose me over her.

Colonel Dad had grown a backbone and stepped in.

The Mother backed down, terrified John'd disown her forever.

"I win! Ha! Japan beats America!"

...Or so I thought.

Because now?

My war prize lies on the couch in Tokyo we can finally afford.

Twenty pounds heavier.

Scratching his belly. Picking his nose. No more fire-breathing butt tricks—he can't lift his legs that high anymore.

This is what I fought so hard for?

I glance at my expired trophy husband and think:

Global harmony?

Eternal justice?

Pfft.

I got played.

It wasn't *me* who snatched him away.

It was *her*—she made me want him.

She made him look rare.

Hard to get.

A treasure.

But now?

I see it.

I didn't win.

I got set up.

And her reign of terror?

Far from over.

CHAPTER 10
THE SECRET TO INTERNATIONAL MARRIAGE

Thud. Thud. Thud.

The footsteps of a drunk monster climbing the apartment stairs echoed through the midnight streets of Tokyo.

Dear neighbors, I'm sorry. But unless I conquer these stairs, I can't go home.

Thud. Thud. Thud.

Ding-dong, ding-dong, ding-dong!

"Okay, okay—quietly now. You'll wake the neighbors,"

John says as he opens the door.

Crash.

The drunk monster collapses face-first in the entryway.

"Gwoooooooooh."

Then John, ever the patient husband, hauls my giant body onto the *tatami* floor and tucks me into the *futon*.

In our house, the gender roles are completely flipped.

The wife rolls in drunk after midnight.

The husband eats dinner alone, cherishing his peaceful solo time lost in computer games, before the hurricane stumbles home.

"You drink too much. It's not healthy,"

John says.

"Idiot,"

I reply.

"If a woman wants to survive in Japan working like a man, she's gotta drink like one too. Haven't you figured that out yet after all your years here?"

That usually shuts him up.

See, John studied Japanese language and culture in college. He prides himself on being a Japan expert.

So when I hit him with a cultural curveball, he suddenly turns all humble and ashamed.

"Wow... there's still so much I don't know about Japan…"

Damn right.

"Why do you insult me in front of people?"

he once asked.

I shrugged.

"Japanese husbands often call their wives "silly" or "foolish" in front of others—even when they're madly in love. It's a cultural thing. We show affection not through praise, but through gentle teasing especially in public."

And just like that, he's nodding, mesmerized.

"Ahh… such deep cultural nuance…"

John drinks sake from a wooden *masu* cup, with salt on the corner like a true old-school Japanese uncle. When he visits public baths, he wears *geta*.

He's so obsessed with being a "Japan insider" that he genuinely believes:

"My wife was born in the Year of the Fire Horse. Of course, she devours men."

Yep. I mentioned this earlier, but I was born in 1966— *Hinoe-Uma*, the Fire Horse, the zodiac sign that comes only once every 60 years.

He's accepted his fate: to be slowly devoured by a rare mythical beast.

"I'm lucky she lets me live,"

he says.

And I think... he actually means it.

My friends ask him,

"John, how do you put up with Megumi?"

And with the pure, innocent smile of a cartoon toddler, he answers:

"Well, she's a Fire Horse. What can you do?"

This, my friends, is how international marriage works.

You respect each other's cultures.

And when you can't understand something?

Just blame it on cultural differences.

See?

International marriage isn't so bad after all.

You hear that, dearest Mother-in-law?

Are you listening?

And your son?

He's still alive.

Smiling.

Loved.

So maybe—just maybe—you were wrong all along.

Are you still listening?

Didn't think so.

CHAPTER 11
THE DEFECTION

"Apparently, this thing will drive Japanese people nuts."

John showed up at Narita International Airport, swinging a tiny paper bag, wearing that familiar dumb grin I hadn't seen in a while.

"What the heck is that?"

Ever since he started working at that mysterious "software" company, he'd been jetting off on endless business trips.

The strange little disc in his little swinging bag? A Japanese-language master of something called *Whatever*-95. I had zero clue what it was. But just a few months later, people were lining up before sunrise, fighting for it like it was the last bowl of ramen on Earth.

The man who used to be my full-time dependent had

returned in triumph—on a business class flight, no less.

"Look at you,"

I said, tears threatening but not falling, like a proud foster parent.

"All grown—landing a real job and everything. I'm impressed."

"Yeah, I guess so," he murmured.

"If this were a drama," I added with a soft laugh, "this would be the happy ending."

"You think so?"

He said it, staring out the window of the airport bus taking us home—his voice flat, his eyes somewhere far away.

What I didn't know—what I couldn't have known—was that he'd already started plotting his next move behind my back.

"Bye-bye, Mother! See you next Christmas!"

The mother-in-law was still an absolute piece of work, but as long as we survived the annual holiday pilgrimage to California, life in Tokyo was blissfully peaceful.

Like I said before, she was terrified of airplanes—convinced flying was unnatural, like birds are suspicious or something—so she'd never come to Japan.

We were finally living like a normal, dual-income, reasonably functional married couple.

We even bought a condo in Tokyo's Setagaya Ward! It was small, and we had a 35-year mortgage, but we were happy. Of course, we didn't tell The Mother.

We were building a life in Tokyo, one step at a time.

As it turns out, John's company was headquartered in Seattle—basically two states above California, where it rains more than it shines.

Every time he traveled there for business, he racked up miles and travel allowances, and I got to party like I was single again, rolling home at sunrise with no one to judge me.

I was living the dream.

Keep working. Keep drinking. Keep earning. Keep Tokyoing forever.

…or so I thought.

"I don't want to be a foreigner anymore."

John said it just as I was cradling a bottle of top-shelf *junmai daiginjo*, debating whether to finish it or leave a few poetic drops for later.

"Sake should be fresh! No regrets!"

I shouted, watching the liquid gold drip into my glass.

"What did you just say?"

I asked, not really looking at him.

John had only been back from Seattle for a few hours. We were supposed to be having a romantic welcome-home feast in our brand-new condo.

And now—what?

He's quitting *being a foreigner*?

Let's be real: with all the dyed hair and imported fashion in Japan, John blended in just fine.

His Japanese was solid.

He understood *wabi-sabi*, *tatemae* and *honne*, *giri,* and *ninjō* (please look them up if you don't know the backbone of Japanese!)—and he didn't even blink at *natto* or pickled squid. Unlike the high-end expats sipping Chardonnay in Azabu, John had actually gone native.

He'd answer the door in polite Japanese whenever religious groups or newspaper salespeople rang the bell. If I shouted from the kitchen,

"Tell them to buzz off!"

He'd calmly reply,

"I'm terribly sorry, but my wife insists,"

while bowing like some refined housewife.

This was a man who'd stand in a bookstore reading cookbooks titled *The Comfort Foods He Misses Most* —then come home and make the eggplant recipe from page 19.

The eggplant had flawless 2mm diagonal slits. The oil, the *dashi*… it was like a Michelin-starred grandma had touched his soul. He'd even chamfer the corners of *furofuki daikon*. I'd never done that in my life.

After seven years in Japan, I thought he'd naturalize, take a *kanji* name, and live forever in Japan.

But then he said it again.

"I don't want to be a foreigner anymore.

I got an offer to work at headquarters in Seattle.

I want to take it."

"Whaaaaaat?"

This was the man who always did what his mom told him.

Then he married me.

So naturally, I assumed he'd just keep doing what *I* said—smooth transition, right?

And now, he had his own opinions?

"I know you have your career," he said gently.

"So I understand it's a complicated decision…"

Damn straight it's complicated.

I have a job. 35-year mortgage. We were settled.

"Is this your mom's idea?"

"No, I haven't told her yet," he said.

"How far is she from Seattle?"

"About 15 hours by car."

"And you still want to go?"

"Yes."

"Is that job really more meaningful than what you're doing here in Tokyo?"

"Yes."

"…You're serious?"

"Yes."

For years, I joked that John was "the most henpecked American in Japan." I assumed he'd do what I said until the day he died. But this? This was a whole new man.

　"… All right then. Go for it."

And just like that, I said yes to Seattle—along with a 30% pay cut. It wasn't a transfer. It meant quitting the Japanese subsidiary and getting rehired from scratch at the headquarters.

"If you hate it, come back. I'll feed you again."

"Much appreciated," he said with a respectful bow.

Our "Welcome Home" dinner turned into a "Bon Voyage" toast.

Just when we thought life was finally settling into something stable, we got thrown into the great unknown again.

Would Seattle be a win?

Would it be a disaster?

Only time would tell.

All I knew was: we were right back where we started.

A long-distance relationship—once between a rice field and a sleek Tokyo office—had gone international.

CHAPTER 12

MISSION: CONCEPTION

"I'll be back Monday afternoon."

"Where are you going?"

"Just heading to Seattle for the weekend."

That's what I'd tell my boss on Friday afternoon as I grabbed my bag and dashed from our Marunouchi office to catch the Narita Express.

If there was a long weekend, you bet I was booking a flight. I flew to Seattle at least once a month—two nights, three if I was lucky.

If I didn't, John and I would've just coasted along in parallel lives… until one day, we quietly forgot each other's names.

Seattle was beautiful—surrounded by mountains, the ocean, and lakes.

Tucked away in one of those peaceful suburbs was the headquarters of the now world-famous software company John worked for. Tech nerds from around the globe flocked there.

And John? He looked perfectly at home among his people.

"How's work?"

"Going well, thanks."

"Any danger of you getting fired?"

"Actually… I'm about to get promoted."

Okay, so Mr. Maybe-I'll-Fail-and-Come-Home was suddenly thriving.

"See you next month!"

We'd enjoy a whirlwind weekend together, and by Sunday afternoon, I was back on a plane, heading straight to work from the airport and onto the Narita Express. At this point, I should probably be on a monthly plan.

Just as I was about to board the plane, John would say it again:

"Why don't you come live here?"

Hmm... That's a problem.

As the plane took off, I sipped bourbon and let it sink in.

There's no doubt—John's career had more momentum in Seattle than it ever did in Japan. I thought he'd bomb and crawl back, but he was doing well.

The problem was, I loved my life in Tokyo. I had a job that made me feel alive.

My office was full of smart, interesting people. In the creative department of an ad agency, no one cared if you rolled in at noon wearing jeans and yesterday's eyeliner—unless there was a client meeting. Then you threw on something vaguely adult.

I went from agency to production company to studio, pitching bizarre concepts like: "What if *tofu* becomes self-aware and rebels against stir-fry?"

Sometimes they even liked it.

I worked with celebrities, ate free bentos, got happily wasted pretty much every night, and cabbed home with no memory. Then I'd chug some hangover cure from the convenience store and do it all over again.

I made nearly double John's salary. The benefits were gold-plated. I could work until sixty and retire with a solid pension. And now I was supposed to give it all up?

But what if I could go to Seattle without quitting...?

—More bourbon.

There was someone who went abroad for an MBA and came back.

Grad school? Me?

Nope.

My brain was marinated in alcohol. No way I was getting accepted. No way I even wanted to study.

So what other kinds of leave did my company offer?

Bereavement... menstrual... maternity…

"THAT'S IT."

A light, boozy epiphany hit me.

"I'M GONNA GET PREGNANT!"

If I got pregnant, I could take maternity leave, plus a full year of childcare leave! That'd buy me a solid year-plus in Seattle. Then I'd just waltz back into the office like nothing ever happened.

Genius.

Forget grad school. No entrance exams, no application essays. Just spread my legs and push—way easier than earning a degree.

"Let's do this!"

So there I was, high above the Pacific, flying solo— warming up my uterus like a prizefighter, with no idea about what I was really signing up for. Just *kiai* and guts, fire blazing, into motherhood.

"I'm off to get the job done!"

Right before the hellish Golden Week travel rush—and on my 30th birthday, no less—I declared this to my boss, fresh off the plane from Seattle.

"What do you need to do this time?"

"Get pregnant! No contraception!"

"Uh... good luck? Or... I honestly don't know what to say…"

My boss, usually unshakable, looked genuinely rattled. I mean, what kind of employee casually declares a baby-making mission? Probably thinking, there's no manual for this kind of employee.

Thanks for always letting me do whatever the hell I want. No way I'm giving up this dream job.

Target locked: Maternity leave.

Mission: No Contraception.

JUST DO IT!

"I've arrived for the job."

I dropped the bomb right there at the airport in Seattle —John had barely said hello.

"Uh... what job exactly?"

He still wanted me to move to Seattle, sure. But become a father? That had not made it onto his to-do list.

Meanwhile, my eyes were blazing. I had never been so... motivated. Funny, considering how little interest I'd shown in this area up to now.

Back at his place, John sat on the bed looking like he'd seen a ghost.

"Well? Are you gonna do this or not? Be clear! Don't you want me to come live here or what?"

"It's just... I mean... I don't think I'm ready to be a dad yet."

"Shut up. This is the only way. Get to it!"

"This is nuts. Don't rush into—oh no!"

Drip.

"Oh noooo! It's out! It's out! What do we do?!"

"Perfect. Mission accomplished. Good job! "

After completing the "operation," I flew back to Narita and straight back to the office. Business as usual.

Naturally, my coworkers were all over me.

"How'd it go?"

"Did you do it?"

"Did it take?"

I'd been a woman for 30 years, but I'd never really bothered to understand things like ovulation cycles or fertility windows. So I called a friend who was well-versed in the art of conception.

According to her, the timing of my trip wasn't ideal at all. Not even close. Bummer. So much for a precision strike.

… But BAM!

Bullseye.

Turns out my hyperactive egg decided to vacuum up one of John's half-asleep little swimmers and defied all logic and science to get the job done.

I picked up the phone and called Seattle.

"Hey! Guess what? We did it!"

"W-w-wait, what? I'm—I'm gonna be a d-d-dad?! I mean, wow, that's amazing! I'm… so h-h-happy… but also completely f-f-freaked out!"

Then it hit me, too.

This guy is going to be a father?

And I'm going to be a mother?

Oh lord.

What.

Is.

Happening.

CHAPTER 13
BIG BELLY OFF TO SEATTLE!

"Hey, you guys, don't you dare smoke in the meeting room!"

"No bento during the meeting? Are you kidding me? No good idea ever comes on an empty stomach!"

Ever since I found out I was pregnant, I'd been picking fights with innocent coworkers left and right—all in the name of protecting my body.

If I didn't eat, I'd puke.

So, whether it was mid-presentation or not, I'd sneak into the bathroom to scarf down a rice ball or sandwich. Or I'd dash into a *soba* stand for a solo slurp session. Whatever my body demanded, I obeyed.

I broadcast my fertility mission loud and clear—so yeah, it wasn't exactly top secret. But for clients and coworkers who weren't in the loop, I just shrugged and said,

"Ugh, must've been one hell of a hangover," and played dumb while skipping drinks at business dinners.

I carried a puke bag, dried sardines (calcium!), and energy bars like some kind of morning sickness survival kit. Even during all-nighters, I worked just like I always did.

Tokyo work life, which used to be my playground, had turned into a minefield for any pregnant woman—and her unborn sidekick.

No wonder Japan's birth rate is in free fall. I wanted to strap a fake belly on some clueless old politician and have him survive my daily commute and smoke-filled meetings.

Plus, work life without booze?

Horrible.

I had been the queen of after-5 p.m. drinking. Now that I was sober—cold sober, the days felt endless. Drunk salarymen on the train looked like wild animals. And honestly? I used to be worse than them.

Living like a decent human is exhausting.

"I should just quit and go to Seattle already."

That's what I told my boss.

"Hang in there a little longer,"

he said.

"You're almost on maternity leave, right? That gives you a whole year off.

And let's be real—someone like you is *not* going to quietly play housewife over there.

If you hate it, you'll come running back.

So just hang tight.

Take your maternity leave, childcare leave, or bereavement leave—whatever's on the HR menu—and treat it like insurance.

If, by some miracle, you end up liking it over there, *then* you can quit."

—This was the same boss who'd always had my back, never raised an eyebrow when I took suspiciously long vacations.

And now? The man sounded surprisingly wise.

What a great company.

For the first time, I actually felt a tiny stab of guilt… for being the booze-guzzling, barely contributing creative hurricane that I was.

So I took his advice to heart.

Hand on my growing belly, I kept working like a solo pregnant warrior.

I powered through till the last minute—then filed for maternity and childcare leave, and waved goodbye to

an office filled with seven years of creative chaos,
hangovers, and laugh-till-you-choke nights.

Pregnant. Headed to Seattle.

I've been shockingly sober for seven whole months.

*And let's be honest—Tokyo's just not the same when
you're not drinking.*

*So I'm off to Seattle to push this baby out like a
champ.*

*I'll be gone for a bit, but once I reclaim something
vaguely resembling*

*my pre-baby figure (lol), I'll be back at the bars—
baby in tow, beer in hand.*

*Until then: wish me luck, send diapers, and save me a
barstool.*

With that cheeky farewell, I left Japan at the end of
autumn, 1996.

CHAPTER 14
PAUSED IN SEATTLE

"*Ittekimasu!*" (I'm heading out!)

"*Itterasshai*" (Take care!)

In the mornings, John would hop into the car wearing the local nerd uniform—faded T-shirt and jeans—and head off to work beaming with joy.

… And what about me?

I was the wife.

But what exactly was a wife supposed to do? I had nowhere to go.

I'd arrived from Tokyo with a giant belly, and in Seattle, I didn't know a single soul.

My only conversation partner was John.

No friends.

Couldn't drive.

Couldn't walk anywhere.

I was essentially under house arrest in our apartment, staring down twelve long, empty hours until John got home.

"Heeeeelp!"

My schedule—once packed tighter than a Tokyo subway—was now a blank page.

John's schedule was filled to the brim.

Unfair.

Desperate, I called a production company back in Tokyo.

"Hello! Got any freelance work? Time difference makes me extra efficient!"

Of course, no jobs came through right away. I was left with… absolutely nothing to do.

Back in Tokyo, I'd spent all my time trying to dodge work. Now I was begging for it.

What is this madness? This anxiety that I had to do something, be doing something, look like I'm doing something?

"I bet Tamura is sipping a coffee in the office café right about now."

"I bet Ohashi is fighting for a taxi to get to the client meeting."

I calculated Tokyo time and imagined my coworkers' day. I'd never known this kind of emptiness.

Is this what retired old men feel like?

Is this the "stay-at-home wife" life?

"Housewife"—a word I never imagined would apply to me.

Back in Tokyo, my neighbor Mayumi was a full-time housewife—a stunning former flight attendant who looked runway-ready even when taking out the trash. Hair flawless. Full makeup. Always in a nice outfit. We were the same age, but she had a two-year-old kid.

I used to think:

She must be bored out of her mind not working every day. What does she even do all day?

I figured—not much.

Every morning, as I stumbled out the door, hungover and half-conscious, Mayumi would wave at me and see me off. I could feel her perfectly manicured judgment burning into my back.

Her unspoken thoughts?

Must be nice having somewhere to go every day.

Don't forget—I was a glamorous flight attendant who once dated celebrities.

I didn't wait in the immigration line like a commoner— I strolled through VIP.

But now… I get it.

She was probably lonely, too.

When you have nowhere to go, no title, no role to play —it's easy to lose yourself.

And now, that's me.

Except... this is America. And I'm still me.

No outings = no shower.

No shower = no clean clothes.

So there I was—braless, in baggy sweatpants, bird's nest hair, sipping decaf coffee on the apartment deck overlooking the lake.

"Damn, that's good coffee."

Never had a cup that tasted this good, even in our over-priced Tokyo condo in Setagaya.

Cheap beans. Decaf. And yet, it was divine.

Why?

Because, for once in my life, I had time to actually taste it.

No distractions. No worrying about the slide order for tomorrow's client pitch. No frantic countdown to catch the 9:58 a.m. train.

Just me, my coffee, and a mind blissfully free of clutter.

It was luxurious.

I gave my whole soul to that cup of coffee.

Back in Tokyo, the hotshot creative from Tokyo University once said of my maternity leave:

"If I had a break like yours, I'd write a novel."

Nah.

Not me.

I'm doing nothing.

New life goal: mastering the fine art of doing absolutely nothing.

When I poop, I poop.

None of that "might as well pee too" multitasking.

I now honor each bodily function's individual journey.

I'm slowing down—on purpose.

I made *chawanmushi*—egg custard's savory Japanese cousin—and learned you're supposed to strain the eggs for a silky texture.

I baked bread and realized: humidity changes everything.

I watched the sun set over the lake—20 minutes, 30... until it disappeared. I never knew sunsets could look like this. I'd never even noticed.

In Tokyo, I drowned everything in booze.

Work. Work. Work.

"No sleep lately!" was worn like a badge of honor.

We mistook overwork for success.

"STOP."

That's what the baby in my belly whispered.

"Enough."

It hit the brakes on life. I was too scared to stop on my own.

I came to America—belly first—and landed in a town so slow, it made Tokyo feel like a fever dream.

John's Seattle apartment.

Foreign pots. Foreign cups.

Nothing familiar.

Just new days.

A brand-new me.

It felt like starting over at age thirty—and this time, I was the foreigner.

John had passed the baton.

His paycheck had shrunk.

We still had the Tokyo condo mortgage.

And a baby is on the way.

But in exchange, I got freedom.

And the thrilling chaos of a life with no script.

Thus began my one-year-only adventure as a foreign, jobless, pregnant housewife in America.

CHAPTER 15
1.2.3 BORN TO REMEMBER

"John! Go get me double cheeseburgers. Fries. And a shake. Now!!"

"Isn't that... a bit much?"

"Shut it. You're not the one who's pregnant— no opinions allowed."

Spending the final stretch of pregnancy in America? Absolute heaven. A paradise for pregnant women.

"My dear, eat whatever you feel like. Stress is worse than calories,"

said my American OB (obstetrician) with a saintly smile.

Back in Japan, every checkup felt like a trial.

The moment I stepped on the scale, my Japanese OB looked at me like I'd committed a crime. I even skipped meals to dodge a scolding. That scale was my mortal enemy.

And don't get me started on the guilt-tripping:

"Pregnancy is not an excuse to overeat!"

Yeah? Tell that to my hormone-fueled, burger-craving body.

Compared to that nightmare, this was pure bliss.

When I asked my American OB,

"So… Do we do enemas before delivery here?"

He raised an eyebrow.

"Do you want one?"

Okay. That definitely sounded weird. Like, I was into that sort of thing. I quickly explained,

"No, no—it's just standard practice in Japan."

Now he looked horrified.

"That's not for the mother's benefit. It's for the doctor's convenience."

Then, with the calm of someone who's seen it all, he added:

"Whatever comes out, we won't be shocked.
No enema needed."

God bless American obstetrics.

And their chill.

My due date was January 24.

But nope—I was determined to give birth one day earlier.

Why? Because January 23 = 1-2-3.

Un, deux, trois.

Uno, dos, tres.

Ichi, ni, san.

Easy to remember in any language, anywhere in the world. Universal, catchy, and probably lucky.

With a birthday like that, my kid was clearly destined for greatness—showers of gifts, a life of abundance. Even John, who couldn't remember my birthday or our wedding anniversary, would *definitely* remember 1-2-3.

This, I decided, would be my very first act of motherhood:

Gift my child the perfect, unforgettable 1-2-3 birthday.

I stared at my belly and sent a psychic message straight to my uterus:

"Let's go, January 23rd. You got this."

"If you've got a preferred date, we can break your water,"

said my ever-chill OB.

Nope.

This had to be natural.

No shortcuts. A pure, cosmic alignment with the perfect date—**1-2-3**.

Only one problem: The baby was in no rush. Clearly enjoying the all-inclusive spa experience inside me. Too comfy to vacate. But if this kid didn't get moving soon, we'd miss the magic number.

"No cheating,"

I told myself.

"But I HAVE to give birth on January 23rd."

"Naturally!"

So, on the night of January 22nd, I launched a one-woman labor operation.

I'd heard the old wives' tales—nipple stimulation, spicy food, wild sex, frantic stair-climbing…basically a to-do list from hell.

Me? I went full freestyle.

Acrobatic squats. Legs flailing. Some kind of primal fertility dance. (Do NOT try this at home.)

John peeked around the corner, horrified.

"Didn't the doctor say not to do stuff like that?"

"Shut up! I'm giving birth to this baby TOMORROW. ONE! TWO! THREE!"

Fueled by stubbornness and decaf espresso, I stomped around the apartment like a possessed *sumo* wrestler. The floorboards groaned. The neighbors probably prayed.

And then—*Drip.*

Wait…

Did I just pee a little?

Or was that…?

Could it be…?

WATER. BREAKING.

"Look! Something's leaking!"

I yelled, pointing dramatically at my crotch. John leaned in to investigate—because my belly was the size of a small moon, and I couldn't see anything past the bump.

"That's not your water breaking,"

he declared.

"They said it gushes—like when you knock over a jar of pickles. That's... just pee."

Pee?! Just pee?!

The audacity.

I'll show you, you jerk. The real flood is coming—just wait!

So I bounced harder. Shook louder. Willed that baby out like a woman possessed.

—That was 10 p.m. on January 22nd.

Still unsure if it was amniotic fluid or just my bladder giving up, I slapped on a pad and went to bed.

The next morning—

January 23rd—the day I'd been training for.

Still felt... a trickle.

Was I just peeing myself again? Oh, the glamour of impending motherhood.

"Excuse me, but I think my downstairs is... leaking."

That's what I told the nurse over the phone.

My chill OB said,

"If you're worried, come on in."

"All right then, might as well."

John, who had an early meeting, sighed—like, *Great. Now I have to escort this maybe-pee-maybe-baby woman to the hospital.*

Tough luck—because guess who still didn't have a driver's license?

I had planned to inhale a massive bowl of fried rice and leftover *gyoza* for breakfast. But in my rush, I grabbed a sad little bagel instead—and off we went.

And guess what?

I was right all along.

Take that, Mr. "It's Just Pee."

It was amniotic fluid, thank you very much.

Shout-out to Japan's high-performance sanitary pads with ultra-absorbent mesh lining.

Apparently, they inspected the pad I handed them—yes, I had to hand a stranger my used pad—and either through scent or science, they confirmed: this liquid was legit.

Yeah!.

"If your water broke at 10 p.m. last night," the nurse said,

"We need to deliver the baby within 24 hours to prevent infection."

Infection from what? No idea. But that was it. I was officially admitted for induced labor.

Nailed it!

I fist-pumped the sky.

I did it.

I cracked the code.

This kid was going to be born on 1-2-3 after all.

A lucky child destined for a rich, memorable life, with a birthday no one could forget.

They hooked me up to IV Pitocin and laid me in bed. The 1-2-3 birthing was officially underway.

Finally, I was going to give birth.

And finally, I was going to drink.

Nine long months.

The moment had come to chill the beer.

Tucked in my hospital bag were two sacred bottles of Redhook Brewery beer, each marked in thick black Sharpie: **"MEGUMI'S. DO NOT TOUCH."**

I'd been fantasizing about this moment for months— popping one open, straight from the hospital fridge, the second that baby left my body.

Just the thought made me salivate. And now? I was starving too.

"Excuse me, when's lunch?"

I asked a nurse, genuinely excited—this was my first-ever hospital stay, and I couldn't wait to see what the hospital meal would be like.

The nurse gave me a kind, almost pitying smile.

"Oh, sweetie, now that we've started inducing labor, you won't be eating again until after the baby comes."

"Whaaaaaaat?! Are you kidding me?!"

Why didn't anyone say that earlier?! I would've eaten a full feast before I let them hook me up to the IV!

So I spent the next several hours riding out contractions with nothing but ice chips, water, and those sad excuse-for-food popsicles—while my glorious fried rice and leftover *gyoza* sat waiting for me at home.

In America, epidurals are the norm.

At the maternity class I attended after moving here, there were over ten couples. Only two of us had decided to go natural—me and another woman. We both had the kind of sturdy, sporty frames that screamed, "We can take it!"

Everyone else in the class stared at us like we were nuts.

"Why would you choose pain if you don't have to?"

"Are you stupid? Or just into suffering?"

Probably both, they thought.

I wondered if that other warrior woman was enduring the same pain somewhere right now.

But hey—I'm Japanese.

And this is what Japanese moms say:

> "You're my precious child because I went through the pain of childbirth to bring you into this world."

It's basically a cultural guilt trip, passed down through generations. And I wanted to say it, too.

I wanted to know exactly what that pain felt like.

I wanted to earn the right to pass on this time-honored, emotionally manipulative gem of maternal love—even if I was doing it in English, across the Pacific.

The glamorous former flight attendant Mayumi I mentioned earlier, used to say it all the time:

"If I hadn't gone through the painful labor to have her, there's no way I could've put up with this little gremlin."

She was talking about her daughter, who, unfortunately for her, looked just like her dad.

My own daughter?

She'd probably turn out even more unfortunate-looking. Stylish? Slim? Definitely not in her destiny.

So I figured I'd better suffer seriously in labor—or I might just abandon the whole parenting gig altogether.

"Pain? Bring it on!"

That's why I had gone in all smiles like some smug pain enthusiast:

... I had not, however, accounted for being tethered to an IV drip, pumped full of Pitocin, and stripped of all freedom—including the right to wander around and pee in peace.

The delivery room was huge and luxurious.

Through the window, I could see a line of snow-capped mountains. There was even a Jacuzzi in the room. All the medical gear was stylishly hidden in sleek designer cabinets, only to emerge dramatically once the screaming hit its peak. It felt like a five-star hotel—minus the vacation.

But thanks to the IV, I couldn't use the Jacuzzi. No warm bubbles. No floating. No soothing hydrotherapy. Just me—tied to a pole like a leashed dog, writhing in a chic little two-meter radius of hell.

Not quite the birth plan I had imagined. Damn it.

—Oh no. It's coming.

A century's worth of menstrual cramps slamming into

me all at once—like a hundred angry wombs rioting in my belly.

John, sensing his big moment, springs into action with the "hee-hee-hoo" breathing techniques he learned in our maternity class.

"Shut up! Don't touch me! Get away from me!"

I transformed into a feral beast of a pregnant woman and batted him aside like an annoying fly.

Just earlier, the nurse had mentioned that induced natural labor usually brings more pain than a regular natural one.

"GUAAAAHHHHHHH!!! RAAAAAAARRRRRGHH!!!"

—If only I could give up.

If only I could say, "Nope, I'm out," and walk away.

I'd done that so many times in life—ditching things halfway, leaving projects and dreams hanging in the middle. Maybe this was karma catching up to me.

But this time?

No exit. No eject button. No escape.

"PLEASE! Give me the drugs! I want the epidural now! I've changed my mind!"

I clung to the bed rails like a desperate pro-wrestler begging the referee for mercy. But the nurse just shook her head.

"Too late! You're past that point. Now push! Fight!"

And just like that, I was thrown back into the ring—no armor, no backup—just me versus biology.

My face was drained of color. Cold chills rippled through me. My pelvis—poor, innocent pelvis—was being pried open by this tiny creature trying to escape.

If someone measured my hips right now, I swear, they'd probably set a new world record for expanded circumference.

It's coming.

It's real.

It's happening.

Game time!

"All right, now push!"

"UOOOOOOOOOOOOOOAAAAAAGGGHH-HHH!"

A beastly roar.

Like I was excavating the bowels of the Earth.

Since most deliveries here were epidural-smooth and drama-free, the nurses looked positively moved to witness an old-school, full-volume, wild-animal birth in the raw.

"I see hair! You're almost there!"

my OB said.

"If you can see the damn hair, just pull the kid out already!"

Yes, I actually yelled that at my OB—in English, with full conviction.

**"UHHHHHHHHHH!
OOOOOHHHHHHHHHH!"**

My howls echoed through the entire hospital.

I screamed louder with each push, shocked by the sheer power of my own voice.

Poor expecting moms in the rooms nearby probably started rethinking their entire birth plan.

I bet at least a few quietly decided, *You know what? Adoption sounds great.*

"WAAAHHH! WAAAHHH!"

Finally.

The baby was out.

My body collapsed.

My mind went blank.

No tears of joy. No angel choirs.

Just full-body shutdown.

My first words as a brand-new mother?

"Did I poop?"

Without missing a beat, John said:

"Yes. It came flying out. But don't worry—I won't tell anyone."

New dad's very first words.

A sacred moment… slightly soiled.

"Wow, that was a beautiful, easy delivery,"

said my OB—still smiling, still perfectly composed, even though my poop had just made a cameo.

No enema, no shame.

Just flying poop and a smiling OB.

"That was easy?! What the hell does a difficult one look like?!"

I swore then and there—

I'm never doing that again.

Ever.

CHAPTER 16
MILOU THE
WACKADOODLE #1

A baby was born.

And not just any baby—this was a One-Two-Three Baby.

Born on 1/23, a numerically blessed little powerhouse, destined for a life of abundance from the very first breath.

Her name is Milou.

As in: *miru* (見る) in Japanese—to see, to try, to take action.

Don't just stand there and think.

Just do it. Try it. Live it.

Go out and see the World.

That's the spirit behind her name.

Spelled MILOU—a name rooted in Japanese, wrapped in a French ribbon.

What a great name!

The new parents were super happy with their naming talent.

And then...

"WAIT JUST A MINUTE!"

OH NO.

She's coming.

The newly self-declared grandmother from California!

I'd been living peacefully in Seattle for just over two months and somehow managed to forget that she still existed.

But there she was—just 900 miles south—alive, kicking, and ready to roar.

And roar she did.

**"Milou? What kind of name is that?
THAT'S NOT AN AMERICAN NAME!"**

She was livid.

"You should name her Catherine! Or Margaret. Or Elizabeth. Or—"

She expected me to pick a name off her family tree like it was some kind of genealogical coupon.

No way in hell I'm naming my kid after one of your creepy dead relatives.

I'm the one who spread my legs and pushed this baby out!

AND I haven't forgotten what you said about our children.

> "They'll be cross-cultural wackadoodles with no identity!"

Remember that?

And now you're saying our brand-new baby girl is a *wackadoodle* and *un-American*—just because of her name?

Oh please.

Shut that big mouth packed into your tiny little body.

This baby is my creation.

My miracle.

Milou,

One day I'll sit you down and tell you the whole story.

How your grandma called you all sorts of names.

How I sometimes wished you were more me than half me.

How I'm sorry—

but even more than that, how I hope you'll grow up to prove her wrong.

Loud.

Proud.

Go out and see the world, Milou.

That's what your name means.

And that's exactly what you were born to do.

CHAPTER 17
HYBRID FAMILY, NO MANUAL

"Hey, get home. Your daughter just pooped."

It was 6 p.m., and John was still at work.

But I—being the sweet, generous wife that I am—always saved the after-5 p.m. diapers for him.

Equal parenting, baby.

Before giving birth, we took a maternity class together, where they taught us how to raise a baby without help from parents or in-laws.

We even learned how to pump breast milk into a bottle so dads could "experience the joy of feeding."

Talk about teamwork.

In America, dads are woven into parenting before the baby even arrives. Even pro athlete dads aren't skipping the birth. They leave mid-game if they have to. That's the standard. God bless America!

Meanwhile, in Japan?

One of my friends said her OB warned:

> "Don't let your husband in the delivery room—
> he might go impotent after seeing all that."

Seriously?

Japanese OBs are weirdly obsessed with enemas, too.
Remember? What's going on, Japan?

This isn't about impotence or shrinkage.

You made the baby together. You greet the baby
together. You raise the baby together. End of story.

In Japan, there's a tradition for new moms to return to
their parents' home for the birth, where an army of
pros—grandma, aunties, neighbors—wait on her hand
and foot. Meals appear. Laundry disappears. The baby
gets passed around like crown jewels on tour.
Basically, a postpartum spa package.

Sounds dreamy, right?

Except… where's Dad?

Answer: usually back in the city, working overtime,
drinking too much, living it up like every night's a
bachelor party (oh, I knew plenty of those guys at
work!)—and missing the first weeks of his kid's life.
Which means… zero practice. And then—bam!

That gap? Way too brutal!

And honestly, it does no one any good.

Bonding with a newborn better start the second that slippery little human pops out.

Moms are literally manufacturing humans from scratch–-nine long months. And then we produce milk on tap.

The least dads can do?

Literally everything else.

They'll never understand the pain of labor. But this is their chance to step up—don't you dare take it away from them!

Hand them the baby straight out of the delivery room. Let them face the 2 a.m. scream-fests, the 3 a.m. pee fountains and/or poo floods, and the 4 a.m. "why won't this thing stop crying" existential breakdowns.

That way, when they do go back to work, they'll suddenly understand: commuting is a luxury vacation.

At home, they'll gladly become their wife's extra set of arms and legs. Or else.

That's why I refused the easy route.

We were in Seattle, just the two of us—no family, no friends, no backup. And if John was going to be a real father, he needed to get his hands dirty from Day One.

Diaper blowouts? His.

Umbilical cord cleaning? His.

Baby baths with a floppy neck and slippery skin?
All his.

Me? I was the one who gave birth.

I was the dairy department, 24/7.

Everything else? That was his department.

And let's not forget—I was the one working full-time in Tokyo while pregnant. Alone.

No husband running out for pickles and ice cream. No one to puke on during morning sickness.

John didn't witness the gradual, terrifying process of my belly popping out and my belly button turning inside out. He has no idea.

So yeah, I earned the right to strut like I run the place. And turning John into a proper dad? Add that to my job description.

I am the mother.

Hear me roar.

"Hey! What the hell are you doing?"

Another after-5 p.m. love call.

"What do you think I'm doing? Working."

"Oh yeah? And who do you think makes it possible for you to even be there?"

"Of course. All thanks to you, my dear."

"If you don't get your butt home soon, your daughter's butt is getting a rash"

"… I'm flying home as we speak."

And that's how we did it.

No babysitters.

No grandparents.

No random college kid on butt-wiping duty—like the one my mother-in-law actually hired back in her day.

Just us—one screaming baby, one equal diaper at a time.

CHAPTER 18
THE REAL EX-CAREER WIVES OF SEATTLE

♪ *"Boooriiing ~*

My brain is melting ~

Pee pee— poo poo—

Boringggg ~!" ♪

Yes, that was me—composing a brand-new nonsense song every day as I pushed my chubby little clone on the swing at the park.

Remember? I was once a Tokyo copywriter. I'm creative. Award-winning, even.

And yet there I was—Queen of Playground Despair— pushing and humming like a lunatic.

That's when I spotted her.

Tanned. Busty. Dark hair tied back. Pushing a curly-haired girl like a robot—muttering something that sounded more like a curse than a lullaby—

"ポルケナンタ レ クソ タレレ..."

And then it hit me.

She's not American.

She's one of *us*.

I could *smell* it.

I couldn't help myself.

"Hi. Where are you from?"

She blinked, like I'd snapped her out of a trance.

"... Argentina."

Jackpot.

"Let me guess—your husband works at M Corporation?"

"What?! How did you know?"

"Because mine does too. We're the same. I felt it."

We locked eyes like war veterans who'd just realized we'd fought the same brutal battle—the battle of identity-erasure-by-expat-marriage.

Then she unloaded:

"I used to be a graphic designer. Big agency. Killer projects. Then boom—husband decides we're moving to America. So I quit, got pregnant, and figured this would be fine. But this? THIS is not fine. You feel me?"

Feel you?

Girl, I want to get matching tattoos.

From that day on, I started treating the park like LinkedIn. I hunted moms like talent scouts chase athletes—sniffing out fellow restless outsiders.

I found quite a few of my people:

>—Luisa, 31, UK:

>"I passed the bar, landed a job. Then *poof*— Seattle. Now I wipe snot and stress-eat."

>—Anita, 35, Hong Kong:

>"I was a trader. Now I trade my soul for nap time."

>—Isabella, 34, Austria:

>"Pastry chef. And now I live in a country where chocolate is a crime."

>—Nicole, 32, Germany:

>"Russian interpreter. Then one drunken night... surprise!"

Seattle weekday parks?

A gold mine.

Talented yet under-stimulated foreign moms. Everywhere. They came from boardrooms. From newsrooms. From design studios. From trading floors.

Back home, we were *somebody*. Not just "wives."

We were trees with deep roots, thick trunks, branches stretching toward the sky.

We had plans. We had momentum. We had identities.

Then—bam.

Husbands announced, "We're moving to America!"

And just like that—*timber!*

Roots gone. Careers gone. Independence—gone.

We landed in America empty-handed. Many of us carried visas stamped: *Not allowed to work.*

"What the hell happened to me?"

And every foreign mom I met said the same thing:

"My husband is chasing the American Dream while I'm stuck wrestling poop and pee. What am *I* chasing? Who even am *I*?"

—Tell me about it. I've got the poop stains to prove it too.

Back home, each of us had sworn:

I'll be a good wife. I'll support him. I'll try this homemaker thing in America—it might even be nice for a while.

Cut to reality: turns out, none of us were built for it.

Yes, babies were always part of the plan.

And with no jobs to fill our days, we thought:

Now's the time. Why not?

So we leaned into motherhood, convinced it would be the grand solution.

Then the baby arrives.

And guess what?

We love them—yes. Adore them—yes.

But our brains? Absolutely starving.

Seattle itself? Gorgeous. Ranked one of the most "livable" cities in America.

For women who dreamed of being full-time moms, Seattle was paradise. A perfect place to raise kids. Jackpot.

But not for us.

We didn't want to spend our days staring at lakes.

Give us the rush-hour trains—where we shared sweat like it was community property.

We wanted presentations. Deadlines. The high-pressure rollercoaster of panic and payoff.

That's what made us feel alive.

Beer tastes best *after* work, not between diaper changes.

Retirement is sweet *after* decades of labor, not before you've even hit 35.

We weren't ready for that kind of paradise.

Yes, we gave our babies 100 percent.

But we had another 100—reserved for work, ambition, the grind our husbands chased every day.

I knew I shouldn't say it.

I told myself, *Don't say it. Don't say it.*

And then—boom—out it came. At least once a week:

> "Stuck here like a single mom? Fine—I"ll do it back home, you bastard!"

—But it wasn't just me.

You could hear it shouted in German. In Portuguese. In Mandarin. Different languages. Same punchline.

We—the foreign moms with heavy English accents— bonded the only way outsiders know how.

No family nearby. Husbands in IT, working brutal hours.

We covered for one another—dentist visits, haircuts, or twenty sacred minutes to drink a coffee while it was still hot.

In that sisterhood, we kept each other afloat.

And then came the question from my tribe:

"Are you going back?"

—Remember my plan?

Get pregnant, spend a year here, then waltz back into my Tokyo office like nothing happened?

I had a desk waiting in Tokyo.

And a boss—long-suffering saint that he was—probably counting down the days until his nightmare copywriter burst in late, armed with the dumbest baby excuse ever invented.

—Am I going back?

Deep in my bones, I knew from the day I gave birth that I couldn't just take Milou and return to Japan. Because John was a good father. A good partner. And no matter how frustrated I was, I couldn't rip that away from him—or from her.

I dreamed a hundred times of striding back into that office, baby photos in hand, ready to wreak havoc all over again.

—But it won't happen.

So forgive me, boss.

Your hopeless, troublemaking copywriter is gone for good.

I'm staying here—with my tribe of foreign moms.

On Milou's first birthday—the day my childcare leave expired—I quit my job in Tokyo.

I cried.

I loved that job. That desk. That version of me.

But it was time.

Not to "settle."

Not to "retire."

To rebuild.

Our roots—ripped out by our husbands' American Dreams—were left exposed, gasping.

But exposed doesn't mean dead.

Like seeds scattered across distant lands, we were planted in foreign soil.

And like those seeds, we are meant to grow—strong, rooted, alive.

One day, we'll bloom again—louder, bolder, brighter.

With my tribe of brilliant, tough, and quietly plotting-their-comeback women beside me, I would chase the dream—with them.

Our dream.

Our American Dream.

And when we catch it?

Our husbands better be ready to eat our dust.

CHAPTER 19
DOT-COM MAMA RISING

Once again today, two-year-old Milou—now fully embracing her dramatic era—collapsed on the floor… just short of making it to the toilet.

As I hand-washed yet another pair of Hello Kitty underwear—still haunted by the ghost of something unholy—I silently cursed my existence.

"I can't take this anymore. This is not a life."

I was now a fully certified, unemployed immigrant mama in Seattle.

Every once in a while, emails would trickle in from my old coworkers in Tokyo:

"Ugh, another all-nighter. Living off canned coffee and cup ramen. I wanna escape to Seattle and chill!"

"Yamada got promoted to creative director! He even won an award for that new ad!"

I'd read those messages while my daughter, snoring like a pug with sleep apnea, lay beside me.

On the glowing screen: Tokyo, moving on without me.

And my reply?

"Don't overwork yourselves! Seattle's great—come visit anytime!"

What a joke.

The truth is, I didn't want anyone to see me like this. I was knee-deep in the no-makeup, no-bra, elastic-waist-band lifestyle.

One day, I want them to see me again—really see me.

Just… not like this.

Not yet.

Dear daughter, I beg you.

Please just start using the toilet like a functioning human.

As I scrubbed yet another soaked pair of Hello Kitty underwear, the phone rang.

> "Hello? Are you the one writing for the local Japanese paper?"

—A strange voice came through the phone.

Uh-oh. That's it. They found me.

See, I was secretly writing a monthly column for the local Japanese-language free paper in Seattle.

I had pitched the column myself. Got the gig. One article a month, thirty bucks a pop. Yes, only thirty. Three-zero.

But I wrote like I was still handling million-dollar clients back in Tokyo.

Every column was sharp, snarky, borderline Rated R. I unloaded all my immigrant-mama frustration in the kind of language that would get bleeped out on Japanese TV.

It became weirdly popular. But I *never* admitted I was the one behind it.

Why?

Because I lived in fear. Fear of being publicly scolded:

"Shame on you! You've embarrassed all of Japan!"

Fear of raw eggs flying at my door. Worse yet:

"You've dishonored your people! Your daughter is hereby banned from Japanese school!"

I wanted her to attend Japanese Saturday school some-day, so I kept a low profile. Shrank my XL presence into a S-sized whisper. Hid my identity at all costs.

"Excuse me?"

I replied, pretending not to understand her question. Maybe if I played dumb long enough, she'd hang up.

But no—this woman wasn't an egg thrower. She works for a brand-new startup in Seattle.

She said,

"I'd love to introduce you to our team and talk about a collaboration."

Wait. What?

Was this... my second act calling?

It was the summer of 1999—

The summer the world found out that Nostradamus was full of crap.

His big prophecy—"*In July 1999, the world will end*"—turned out to be a total bust.

I secretly believed him.

Who needs to repay loans if there's an apocalypse? Who needs skincare? I figured wrinkles would die with the rest of humanity. And why count calories when the asteroid was going to hit before swimsuit season?

But guess what? The bills kept coming. The wrinkles multiplied. And my tummy? It developed a personality of its own. Turns out, the world didn't end—just my metabolism.

So when it became clear the apocalypse had been canceled, I had to start thinking seriously about my future—

BAM.

That call.

That strange, unexpected call from some startup. You bet I wagged my tail and followed.

And guess what?

They were about to launch a brand-new internet portal —think Yahoo!, but pinker—targeted at young women in Japan. And they wanted me to write a column for it.

Was this real?

After months of scrubbing poop out of Hello Kitty underwear, was this my karmic reward?

Thank you, God. Thank you, Buddha. Thank you to whatever deity is currently in charge of moms with crushed dreams and poopy hands. I hadn't felt this alive since... Well, honestly, who even remembers?

But then I realized—hold on.

A website for *Japanese ladies*?

Oh honey. That's not some cute little side hustle. That's a war zone.

Back in Tokyo, I worked on women's products, and let me tell you, marketing to young Japanese women? Not for amateurs.

These girls are sharp. Trend-hungry, brand-loyal—for about a week. Richer than you'd expect, pickier than a Michelin inspector, and constantly in search of whatever's "next." They're basically emotional stock markets in platform shoes.

No offense, but American marketers don't know what the hell they're doing with that demographic. You can't just slap some glitter and toss them a 10% off coupon.

So I thought,

First order of business: educate these American folks about the wild jungle that is the Japanese consumer market.

Armed with my war stories from Tokyo, I marched into that company like I was on a divine mission.

At the time, Seattle was in full-blown dot-com fever. Everyone and their dog was launching a startup. Retired engineers who'd cashed out big with stock options from major tech companies were suddenly venture capitalists, tossing money at anything ending in ".com" like they were feeding pigeons at a park.

The company I walked into was one of them—its management team was just a bunch of engineer dudes who one day looked around and went,

"Japan seems... profitable?"

And voilà—instant Japan-focused dot-com startup!

No plan. No research. Just vibes.

Of course, none of them spoke Japanese. None of them had ever been to Japan. These guys didn't just underestimate the Japanese market—they couldn't even spell it.

I was furious.

ARE YOU KIDDING ME!? You think you can just point at Japan on a map and cash in?

These nerdy cowboys needed a serious education.

And guess what? Class was in session. I crashed the scene—whiteboard ready, pointer aimed, and verbal sniper mode fully activated.

"Look at this!"

I reached into my bag and pulled out... a Japanese sanitary pad.

Then, right there in the conference room, in front of the CEO, the CFO, and a parade of pale, under-caffeinated tech bros—I gave them a live demo of its engineering brilliance.

Rip.

One pull and the packaging opened like a flower.

Snap.

Three adhesive tabs release in perfect harmony. And the trash? Neat, compact, and totally mess-free.

"This—THIS—is Japanese marketing!"

Silence.

All eyes were locked on the pad, now resting like a sacred artifact in the middle of the conference table. They stared, stunned.

Who is this woman?

Is she really Japanese?

Aren't they supposed to be... I don't know... smaller?

Quieter?

Sorry, bros, what you got is a six-foot-tall human megaphone with a sanitary pad demo and a mission to enlighten.

"Japanese tech is all about precision, efficiency, and customer obsession. Even our pads are high-performance.

You want to impress Japanese women? You'd better bring your A-game. They don't mess around."

Still, no one spoke.

Their eyes remained glued to the pad. You could see the panic swirling.

Which side is up...?

Does the sticky part go on the... no, wait...oh god, that would hurt...

Their inner monologues were clearly in chaos. The existential dread began to sink in.

What were they doing trying to launch a startup targeting Japanese women?

They weren't ready.

They were never ready.

And just like that—BAM—my Japanese sanitary pad had done what a thousand PowerPoints never could: Strike fear into the hearts of cocky IT bros.

Mission accomplished.

"Boys, relax! With me on your team, you've got a hundred million horsepower!"

I channeled my inner American and did what any over-confident start-up bro would do: I oversold myself.

"You want branding? I got it.

Need copy? I'll write till your servers melt.

Marketing? I'll sell *tofu* to cowboys."

I pitched like one of those Americans who claim they're fluent in Japanese—but can barely order sushi.

And these poor tech guys? Still in shock from the Surprise Sanitary Pad Showdown, they were in no state to think rationally.

They weren't hiring me—they were clinging to me like I was the last match in a blackout.

You could see the gears turning:

If she leaves, we're doomed. She knows the market. She knows… biology.

And then—

"We'd like to offer you the position of VP of Marketing."

"Heck yeah! I accept it! Leave all things menstrual to me!"

I never thought I'd land a job in America.

I barged in for a freelance gig and walked out as a Vice President.

That's right—Vice Freakin' President.

At a dot-com startup.

In the late 90s.

I was *back*, baby.

Goodbye, poop-pants toddler life.

Hello, grown-up office chat, client calls, and business trips to Japan. Real clothes! Real conversations that didn't involve Hello Kitty or Elmo!

It was the comeback of the century.

All thanks to a cheeky little column I'd been writing for thirty bucks a month.

Sometimes, all it takes is a good bluff and a precision-engineered Japanese pad.

CHAPTER 20
STARTUPLAND CIRCUS

"WAAAAAAHHHH!! BIEEEEEEHHHH!!"

Welcome to Narita International Airport.

Another glamorous international business trip—with a toddler who'd clearly been possessed by jet lag… and maybe something darker.

"Stop crying already! If you don't walk by yourself, I'm leaving you here!"

There she is, face-down on the floor, kicking and screaming like she's auditioning for *The Exorcist: Toddler Edition*.

Happens every time. Yes, I'm now a venture-backed business mama. Flying to Japan *every single month*. Power moves!

But of course, I'm not flying solo—I'm dragging my screaming sidekick along.

As other passengers exit gracefully, my child shapeshifts into a full-blown Tasmanian devil, flailing all four limbs like she's trying to summon a portal to hell.

I don't blink. I walk straight to the customs line. No engagement. No negotiation. You scream in protest? You face the consequences. Mommy's justice is swift.

People gape. Some look concerned. Others are horrified.

I keep marching, shouting over her wails. She ups the volume. It's Godzilla vs. Mothra—except Mothra's in Hello Kitty leggings and screaming,

"MAMAAAAAA!"

The customs officers look visibly rattled.

"Um… is it okay to just leave her behind like that?"

"She didn't walk. She chose the floor. She can cry here for eternity."

My daughter screamed like her life was over.

"EHHHHH! NOOOOO!"

One officer nearly faints. My daughter bolts over. Then he waves us through—like he's hoping we'll leave before I blow something, verbally or otherwise.

"Go ahead, ma'am. And sweetie, maybe listen to your mama next time, okay?"

Even the guy at the automatic doors chimes in.

"Where to, ma'am? Let me push that for you."

Everyone just wants us *gone*. Yes, we are *that* annoying. And yet—despite the mayhem, the chaos, and the shrieking—this mother-daughter wrecking crew flies into Japan. Every. Single. Month.

Doing a startup with a toddler? Let me tell you— brutal. This wasn't some neat little 9-to-5 gig. It was a full-blown, 24/7, sleep-deprived, jet-lagged, budget-blowing circus.

But still—every day brought electric stimulation.

I wasn't just "Milou's Mommy" anymore. I was a functioning member of adult society! A real human with a title, an email signature, and finally—no more living in elastic pants.

If I hadn't been trapped in toddler poop and pee for those few years, I don't think I could've appreciated this rush.

Like a freshly released ex-con pledging to go straight, I was fired up to rejoin society, burning with purpose and gratitude.

"Back again, huh?"

"So… when are you leaving *this* time?"

My mother's welcome back home grew colder with each return trip. Can't blame her. Every month, I crash-landed into my parents' house like a typhoon, dropped my toddler on them like a sack of potatoes, and vanished—sometimes overnight. Honestly, they were saints for not changing the locks.

April 2000—The site was set to go live.

Big-time debut. Major launch. Cue the trumpets! But until then? Pure chaos.

Content had to be created. Marketing strategies had to be executed. A whole damn team had to be built from scratch in Japan.

And all of it had to happen—yesterday.

This wasn't like the old days at the fancy ad agency. Back then, I walked into client meetings like a queen in heels.

Now? I was more like a sketchy door-to-door sales-person pushing a no-name startup with a weak logo and a weaker budget.

The Tokyo "office"?

It was in a dingy mixed-use building a few train stops past Shinjuku. Three dream-filled young guys had made it their home base, ready to gamble their youth on a startup jackpot.

Keeping their spirits up? Also, my job.

"Let's eat!"

"Let's drink!"

"Let's *karaoke*!"

We did everything together. We worked our butts off. Then we drank till morning. Sang like it was our one shot to impress the gods—or at least the neighbors.

When our voices were completely shot, we'd crawl back to the office just in time to sync with the Seattle office, where the sun was just rising.

"Hello?"

"Whoa—you sound awful. Are you sick?"

"Maybe... but we've got too much work to do... I'll power through... *cough cough.*"

Oscar-worthy performance. Let the Americans think we were warriors of productivity and sacrifice.

In the corner of our office sat a *kotatsu.* Yeah, a heated table someone had literally dragged in off the street.

At night, we all jammed our legs under it and collapsed into sleep. The floor trembled as dump trucks rumbled down the highway outside.

The air buzzed with the scent of dreams, cup noodles, and unshowered ambition.

In Seattle, our fearless CEO Bryan, and the founding team were hustling for funding, while the tech squad built the actual site. Meanwhile, I was in Japan running around screaming at printers, PR firms, and at anyone to "KEEP THE FIRE BURNING!"

Yes—me. Transpacific motivational speaker. Chief cultural translator. Emergency duct tape for every leak in the startup boat.

But, wait—

> "Can people who don't speak Japanese really build a Japanese site... in Seattle?"

> "Why is the target audience in Japan, but the website is being built 4782 miles away?"

These thoughts bounced around in my head.

As the one doing the monthly ping-pong between Japan and the Pacific Northwest, I was starting to feel the pain of long-distance startup life.

Slow responses.

Miscommunications.

Finally, I said what I was thinking:

> "Is this... even okay?"

Bryan, unfazed as always, hit me with the classic founder gospel:

> "That's the beauty of startups.
>
> We do what big companies *can't*.
>
> Flexibility is our edge.
>
> Speed is our secret sauce.

Don't overthink.

Just run.

Run at **internet speed!**"

Run where? Run how?

Nobody knew.

But we ran blind, panicked, caffeinated—at so-called *internet speed.*

Whatever the heck that means.

Maybe I was still clinging to my old corporate brain.

Maybe while I was off giving birth and scrubbing poop out of Hello Kitty underwear, the world had sprinted past me in wireless sneakers.

Maybe the very things I didn't understand were exactly where the startup gold was hiding.

Yes.

That had to be it.

Don't think—run!

This bizarre beast called "startup business"…

I had no idea what I was doing.

A total startup virgin.

Naïve. Hopeful.

And the more I let myself believe,

"Because it's a startup!"

—was a legitimate excuse for literally anything—the deeper I sank into the beautiful, chaotic quicksand of Startupland.

The more I told myself,

"This is fine."

Spoiler: It wasn't.

CHAPTER 21
LOST IN TRANSLATION –
AND FOUND MY SENSES

"The train's at the platform, and the doors are about to close!"

"If we don't jump in right now, we're getting left behind!"

Great metaphor.

One of our younger Japanese teammates was practically foaming at the mouth, so hyped he could barely stay in his chair.

Dot-com fever had officially hit Japan, and we were still stuck at the gate.

"Move at internet speed!"

Bryan—our fearless CEO—kept yelling like a startup Napoleon charging into battle.

So we did.

We sprinted.

We gasped.

We hurled ourselves at deadlines, powered by caffeine and pure chaos.

But no matter how hard we pushed forward, something kept yanking us back. Like trying to cross a busy street with someone clamped onto your ankles.

"Who's slowing us down?!"

I turned around—and there they were: Bryan and the Seattle HQ crew, grinning proudly, reins in hand.

They didn't speak Japanese. They didn't know the culture. Yet somehow, they were still driving the bus.

Naturally, we were lost.

The website built by the Seattle crew was a glorious disaster. Garbled characters everywhere—like alien symbols.

And the content we'd painstakingly crafted in Tokyo, with actual Japanese professionals? The Seattle devs would just casually "adjust" it.

If I had a developer next to me, I would've smacked his arm and said, "Fix this. Now."

But no.

Instead, I had to send desperate emails across the Pacific.

By the time my message floated across the ocean, slid into their minimalist office, and popped up on some laid-back coder's screen...The moment had passed. The urgency evaporated. And so did the context.

And when they finally opened it? Of course, they had no idea what they were looking at. They couldn't tell beautiful Japanese from broken nonsense. To them, the site was either fully functional or some cutting-edge Japanese abstract art project.

No shame. No urgency. No clue.

When it came time to pick a partner for our celebrity gossip section, the Japanese team had already decided unanimously: "Obviously, it's gotta be *Uwasa Queen* (not the real name)!"

Boom. Done. Next!

But nope. Not even close.

To get Bryan's approval, we had to start from absolute zero. Cue a crash course on the entire Japanese media landscape—competitor charts, consumer trends, demographic deep-dives, and probably ending with a TED Talk titled *"Trust Us, We're Japanese."*

All this… just to justify a decision that any Japanese intern would've rubber-stamped mid-onigiri bite.

It was like being forced to eat a bowl of rice using a fork in your left hand and a knife in your right (yep, like my mother-in-law preaches)—just to prove you belong at the table.

A bowl I could usually inhale in three minutes? Now it takes an hour of dainty pecking. And this is what we call *internet speed*?

Please.

In Seattle, young people were lining up to join any shiny new dot-com venture.

Bryan? He just kept hiring them—expanding the company like a balloon animal at a kid's party.

But the moment I said,

"Hey, how about sending one of our web developers to Tokyo?"

They clutched their hoodies like comfort blankets and whined,

"But our *hoooome* is here! You're the one flying back and forth. You deal with it."

And that's when it clicked.

You don't even respect Japanese women. You dangle rewards we'll never get to bite—while we do the grunt work, you daydream about IPOs.

This isn't a startup.

It's a sweatshop in disguise.

And if that wasn't enough, Bryan kept flipping the company's direction like pancakes.

I joined because he said "we're launching a site for Japanese women," so I ran around Tokyo, chasing licenses for women's content—period advice, love horoscopes, the whole girl-power buffet. Then out of nowhere:

"The female market's too narrow. Let's target men too."

NOW you say that?

Then he reads about a mobile startup getting funding, and suddenly it's,

"We're pivoting to mobile!"

Like it's a yoga pose.

Next day:

"Let's drop B-to-C. We're going B-to-B."

Then:

"Forget Japan. Korea? No—Europe! Let's go global!"

Bryan was like a toddler in a toy store—grabbing every shiny thing in sight, totally forgetting what we came in for.

Haven't you heard the great Japanese proverb— "Copycats get the scraps"?

You don't win big by copying.

You win by creating. By having your own damn business model.

But Bryan kept parroting the same startup nonsense:

> "You've got to pivot to keep up with the times!"

Yeah.

Sure.

I swallowed every shift, every irrational demand. Because "that's how startups work."

I blamed myself—maybe I just don't get it. Maybe I'm not experienced enough.

So I kept running.

Kept pushing.

Kept pretending.

But not anymore.

I'm done being Startup Stupid.

I don't even remember what I was chasing anymore. Worse—I dragged real people into this mess. Partners. Clients. My own family. All in the name of "internet speed"?

No thanks.

I stopped running.

I'm out.

CHAPTER 22
CHIEF EVERYTHING OFFICER

After I left, Bryan's company couldn't secure more investor funding and began tilting sideways—at *internet speed*, of course.

Eventually, Bryan got himself fired, the company was sold off to a local firm, and the whole thing fizzled out in the saddest anticlimax imaginable.

The dot-com bubble popped. One by one, the other startups followed.

"See? Told ya startups were a joke."

I could practically hear my old coworkers in Japan smirking across the Pacific.

I wanted to prove them wrong.

I wanted that "Damn, she did it!" moment.

But… nope.

I ran out of steam. The bubble ran out of air.

"You'll crush it next time. You learned so much from this."

That's what my American friends—and my international tribe—told me.

Here, failure isn't shameful—it's a step on the way to something better. Better to face-plant than sit around polishing a dream that never moves.

So fine.

I'll channel my inner American.

Forget the shame. Own the story.

I lost my startup virginity to a total dud. But hey—I got a killer story out of it.

The experience opened my eyes to a different kind of America. I made real connections—not just with immigrant ex-career moms, but with people from all walks of life. I racked up serious mileage. Not a total loss.

My famous after-5 p.m. love calls to John resumed:

"Hey, what are you doing? It's your daughter's bath time!"

"I'm still working…"

"She's going to bed smelly if you don't get home."

"Yes, ma'am! On my way!"

And just like that, I was back in the domestic arena.

I'd ditched my family for a taste of startup glory—but miraculously, they took me back.

No questions. No grudges.

"I quit the company."

That was my big return speech to John.

"Oh. Okay."

That was his entire response.

He was playing it safe. Smart man. After years of verbal *judo* with me, he knew better.

"If you're short on cash, I could go back to work."

"Oh no no," John said, smiling nervously.

"Just having you two at home is more than enough for me."

"Let's be clear—quitting the company doesn't mean I'm crawling back to full-time stay-at-home mom mode."

"Uh… were you ever *really* a stay-at-home mom?"

"EXCUSE ME?!"

"Eep—strike that. I meant: you were amazing. Truly."

Startup or not, the truth is—I love working.

I love being around adults who don't talk about diaper rash and lunchbox hacks.

I love being good at something that has nothing to do with folding laundry or scrubbing poop out of Hello Kitty underwear. (Seriously, how many times now?)

And for the first time, I actually felt like I could do this —work in America.

But go back to being someone else's employee?

No, thank you.

My daughter is precious. My family means more than any meeting, any bonus, any IPO.

I'm no longer that Tokyo wild child who could party all night and crush presentations by breakfast.

My base is here now.

This is where I'm needed most.

And let's be real—without me, John had lost all rhythm.

Some people thrive under pressure. He's one of them —adorably competent, but somehow more efficient with a little fire under him.

So fine—I'll keep lighting the match.

But this time, it's on my terms.

"That's it. I'll become a CEO!"

I mean, if Bryan the Buffoon could run a company, why not me?

Time to be my own boss.

Time to do what I actually want to do.

Strike while the iron's hot? Nah. Incorporate while the iron's hot!

I cleared out my daughter's playroom—out went the dress-up rack, the plastic cupcakes, the pretend kitchen.

> "As of today, this room is now the company headquarters."

I claimed a sunny spot by the window, planted a very official-looking desk, and crowned myself CEO. In the corner sat a wobbly, beat-up desk.

> "From this day forward, address me as CEO."

> "And who gets the broken desk?" John asked.

> "You do. Congratulations—you're our company intern."

> "Ehhhhhh!?"

It was the perfect setup for a happy home life.

I could work, be near my family, and if John needed a motivational butt-kick, I'd be right there.

If my daughter got sick, I'd lie her down next to my CEO chair and nurse her back to health.

And if I wasn't feeling it that day?

Midday nap. Afternoon beer and wine.

No boss. No guilt.

Internet speed?

Screw that.

I'll move at Megumi Speed.

Try to keep up.

I decided to build my own creative house.

Just me, my laptop, and the skills I'd spent years sharpening in Tokyo's ad world.

Plus an unpaid intern—my husband.

Honestly, he's better than those tech bros I used to work with.

No stock options.

No unicorn dreams.

Nowhere near an IPO.

I only take on what I love—columns, bilingual copywriting, marketing for Japanese brands.

Every project is lovingly poked, prodded, and polished until it shines.

Another night, another after-5 p.m. love call—

"What are you doing now?"

"Working. Obviously."

"Come back and put in some real hours at *our* company."

"Our company…?"

"Complain too much and I'm not cooking dinner."

"Yes, sir! Heading home now, boss!"

And just like that—

I'm the CEO, the creative lead, the domestic drill sergeant.

Chief Everything Officer.

Running this little company with big ambition—one lovingly kicked husband at a time.

Business? Totally booming—

in my imagination.

Morale? High.

CEO life? Crushing it.

Now, if only I could get HR to approve my booze budget…

CHAPTER 23
TROPHY WIFE, MY WAY

"Come on in!"

On weekends, I love inviting John's coworkers over for dinner—especially the ones who've openly fantasized about marrying a Japanese woman.

Without fail, the moment I open the door, they flinch.

Whoa.

What is this… towering woman?

Inside the kitchen, the man living their dream—John—is in an apron, frying up tempura.

And his Japanese wife (me)?

Not walking three steps behind him.

Not bowing sweetly.

Nope.

I'm front and center.

Slightly tipsy. Smelling like a sake brewery. Wielding a giant *isshou-bin* (1.8L bottle) like a warrior queen.

"Hey, John! Where's the appetizer?"

"Coming, honey!"

John wipes his hands on his apron and brings out the *edamame*.

The guests freeze.

Confused.

Nervous.

> *Wait… what is this?*
>
> *This is backwards.*
>
> *Upside-down. Un-American. Un-Japanese. Un-everything.*

Then I go in for the kill:

"I don't know how he's doing at work, but at home? I have to whip him into shape. I'm like, 'Speak up! This is America!' He still can't stand up to his mom."

> *Uh-huh…*

"He's basically my dependent. I raised him from scratch."

> *…oh.*

They sip their drinks in silence, scanning the room like they're calculating the distance to the nearest emergency exit.

They came for the fantasy:

A delicate Japanese wife.

Delicate food.

Delicate manners.

What did they get?

A human wrecking ball in lipstick and stretchy pants, yelling over the sound of sizzling oil—not from the kitchen cooking, but from their faces, burning off the sake fumes.

Eventually, they fake a yawn.

"I think I drank too much... gotta go."

"Wait, don't go! We've got *mochi* ice cream!"

John appears with a tray, hopeful.

Too late.

The guests are halfway into their shoes, mumbling about early meetings.

"Come on, let's do one last *kanpai!*"

I raise the bottle.

They run for their lives.

And yet—miraculously—this disaster works in John's favor.

Back at the office:

> "John's wife is a monster."

> "If he's survived that for years, he must be amazing at conflict resolution."

> "He's got leadership potential. Hidden, but powerful."

Boom. His stock rises.

What a supportive wife I am.

I didn't just entertain the guests. I shattered their precious little stereotypes of Japanese women—then served up a brand-new model: bold, bilingual, and spiced with extra attitude.

In their heads, "Japanese wife" means:

Petite. Quiet. Obedient. Endlessly caring.

Just like some Japanese girls grew up dreaming of blond princes, some American boys grew up dreaming of soft-spoken Asian angels.

And I'll never forget this guy from Nebraska—the one who took over John's English-teaching job after he moved to Tokyo. When this guy first arrived in Japan, he threw tantrums like a toddler.

"I hate it here! I wanna go *hoooome*! The food is weird, the weather's gross, the countryside's boring!"

(Nebraska is basically cornfields, but sure, go off.)

He sulked. He pouted. He stomped his big corn-fed feet.

But a few months later?

Whole new man.

> "Japan is amazing! Back home I was a nobody. Here—I'm a star!"

And what flipped the switch?

Not sushi. Not temples. Not cherry blossoms.

It was the girls.

Local sweethearts who swarmed his blond hair and blue eyes like he was some kind of Hollywood heartthrob.

He strutted around town like the King of Rural Japan, cycling through girlfriends one after another. Blink, and he'd upgraded again. And he bragged to his buddies back in Nebraska:

> "Dude, get over here! You'll be worshipped. Total paradise. Do whatever you want!"

—And that, ladies and gentlemen, is the fantasy.

That's the myth so many American guys carry in their back pockets: date a Japanese woman, and you're instantly a rock star.

Which is why I consider it my civic duty—my patriotic calling—to smash that fantasy to pieces.

One dinner party at a time.

So when someone leans in and says,

"I heard you married a Japanese woman?"

John just grins.

"Oh yeah. You should come over sometime."

All right then. I am ready to entertain.

John's in the kitchen, braising eggplant with soy and ginger.

And me?

I'm by the door—sake in one hand, my biggest Japanese smile set to MAX.

"Welcome! Come on in!"

Their face freezes.

Their soul trembles.

　Dar God...what have I walked into?

Just dinner, darling.

With a side of culture shock.

CHAPTER 24
SEATTLE BRANCH UPRISING

"Summer vacation! Everyone, report for duty!"

Once again, the royal decree came down from my beloved mother-in-law.

She does this every year—summer, Thanksgiving, Christmas, Easter, her birthday, even our wedding anniversary.

Somehow, she's appointed herself the family's official travel agent—for life.

And every single time, she finds a destination so bland, so aggressively boring, we're left stunned, asking:

"Wait—this is a tourist destination? In America??"

But never doubt The Tyrant of Travel.

She always delivers.

Her true goal on these trips—every single time: To trap the entire family in one location and declare,

"The world revolves around ME. Don't you forget it!"

It was always the same ritual.

After claiming dominance over the family, she'd retreat for the final flourish—her private little affirmation moment in the mirror.

"Mirror, mirror, on the wall, who's the most powerful woman of all?"

And for years, the mirror answered on cue:

"Why, it's you, Mother."

She lived for that moment—smirking at her reflection like a dictator admiring her own propaganda.

But lately… the script's been changing.

"Mirror, mirror, on the wall, who's the most powerful woman of all?"

"That would be... your daughter-in-law in Seattle."

"WHAT DID YOU JUST SAY!?"

The woman's blood pressure skyrockets. Her royal mirror dares to speak of a new queen rising?

Seattle may be 900 miles away, but apparently the

seismic waves from me simply existing have reached the enchanted mirror realm.

And my dear mother-in-law is *not* amused.

Her precious firstborn may have returned to the U.S. mainland, but—*gasp*—he settled in Seattle.

That's right. The forbidden zone.

The land where her claws can't quite reach. And worst of all… he married me.

Since this rogue "Seattle Branch" was established, the other siblings have started making frequent pilgrimages north—*without her.* And it terrifies her.

"The Seattle Branch must be destroyed."

Like a war general plotting her final siege, The Mother begins a campaign of "California Family Holidays."

The mission: Drain every last hour of her children's PTO (Paid Time Off). Exhaust them. Leave them with zero vacation days to sneak off to Seattle and sip sake with the enemy.

And just like that, we're trapped.

We've been outmaneuvered. By the time we even *think* about planning our own quiet getaway? No PTO. No budget. No hope.

"Operation Mother-in-Law-Free Holiday!"

That became the official slogan of the Seattle Branch.

Step One in reclaiming our independence: Unanimous rejection of her Annual Christmas Hostage Situation.

I told John,

"You have a family now. We need our own traditions. Milou deserves Santa sliding down *our* chimney. We are not traveling anywhere!"

But John was paralyzed. The thought of telling his mother that we were skipping Christmas gave him full-body tremors.

"Pick up the phone!"

I barked, shoving the receiver into his trembling hand.

"If you don't call her, no gaming tonight!"

"Not that! Please!"

That man loves gaming more than life itself. He might look gentle, but in the virtual world, he's apparently a deadly assassin with a body count.

So, yes—John was officially appointed as our Designated Bringer of Disappointment to my dear mother-in-law. All in the name of digital gunfire and family freedom.

"Mom… how are you? …Oh, I see. (*Thud!*) Ow—no, no, nothing. Just, uh… stubbed my toe. So… we've decided that, uh, Santa Claus is officially coming to our house this year. So… from now on… we're, uh, unable to leave the house for Christmas… ever again… indefinitely…"

He actually said it.

And then—The Mother simply said:

"Oh. Okay. Huh."

Click.

John looked stunned.

"She didn't say anything. I think it's fine."

I glared at him.

"You really think she's just going to let it go that easily?"

He puffed up.

"Hey, I laid down the law. I told her straight up."

Oh, sweet, naive gamer husband.

No one just says no to her and walks away unscathed. You might think you survived the ambush. But the sniper's just switching scopes.

The next day, we got her response.

My dear mother-in-law left us a voicemail.

A weaponized voicemail.

> **"I booked a room with a fireplace.**
>
> **There'll be a Christmas tree in the lobby.**
>
> **I've already signed up for Santa photo ops.**

So we're not ruining Milou's dream or anything…

Right?

CHRISTMAS.

PALM BEACH.

BE THERE."

Click.

She didn't argue.

She just made it impossible to say no—with twinkle lights and Santa bait. This woman could teach hostage negotiation tactics at the Pentagon.

What the hell are we supposed to do with this woman!?

"Well… I mean… we kinda have to go, right? I mean, Santa's gonna be there…"

"You idiot! This is why she always wins! Because you roll over like a sad little dog! Milou and I are not going. YOU go. Go have your little mother-son love-fest without us!"

Of course, John didn't have the guts to show up solo. So he started burning through long-distance minutes. (Back then, kids, out-of-state calls were expensive.)

He called up all his siblings and somehow convinced them to form a resistance:

"Milou deserves to spend Christmas at her own home.

With her own chimney.

Waiting for *her* Santa."

And just like that—YES!

Our first-ever family Christmas at home!

No mother-in-law included.

Just us, a tree, and total freedom!

Let her sit by the hotel fireplace and take her hostage —Santa photos with whoever she wants. We're out!

…Or so we thought.

Because, of course, it's never that easy with The Tyrant of Travel.

And then—it happened.

A grand announcement on our answering machine.

"The California Headquarters will be coming to Seattle for Christmas!"

EXCUSE ME!

Didn't we win our family autonomy?!

If John's siblings want to come—fine, whatever— COME ALONE. Why on earth would you bring her with you!?

Answer: Because she's terrified of a Seattle uprising.

She knows it.

We're getting too strong. Too independent.

In her mind, *participation = prevention.*

If she shows up to everything, no one can plan a coup behind her back.

Fine.

Let her come.

But this time… It's MY turf.

Seattle is my territory. You're not running the show up here, lady.

This time, we're locking YOU down.

You're stepping into the one place in America where a Japanese woman runs the show like it's a *sumo* ring in her own damn backyard.

And in my house, we do things *my* way.

Brace yourself, dear Mother-in-law.

This is OUR revolution.

The California Headquarters has arrived for the holiday—

Welcome to the Seattle Branch!

Let's give her the full-blown JAPAN experience she never asked for!

Take off your shoes at the door.

Bow before you enter.

Sleep on a *futon* so thin it'll make your chiropractor cry.

Full Japanese immersion.

Chopsticks only. No forks. No knives. No whining.

Let's see how "tolerant" you are now.

Are we ready?

I'm rolling up my sleeves, letting my upper arms jiggle with pride, and giving the California clan the full-on royal welcome.

It's breakfast time at the Seattle Branch!

Steaming white rice. Piping hot miso soup with seaweed and *tofu*. Stringy *natto* that smells like a haunted foot. And just to be generous, I'll even throw in grilled *shishamo*—those little fish with heads still on and their eyes still judging you.

"Breakfaaaaast is ready!"

I sing out.

My dear mother-in-law freezes.

"*Itadakimaaaaasu* (let us eat)!"

Milou chomps into the *shishamo* head-first like a barbarian warrior. Seaweed dangling from her lips, she slurps miso soup like a pro—loud and proud.

Still no sound from my dear mother-in-law.

Then—angelic voice, full volume:

"Grandmaaa, Mommy's cooking is soooo good!"

Oh, my sweet, sweet girl.

Full-blooded Japan mode: activated.

You see that, woman!?

Your precious American granddaughter? You once said she'd grow up all confused, the cross-cultural wackadoodle with no identity?

Well, guess what—she's bilingual, bicultural, and crushing it.

"Grandma, look!"

Milou gleefully dips her fingers into a gooey mountain of *natto*, pulling up long sticky strings like she's Spider-Man at breakfast.

She leans in, proudly dangling the fermented threads just inches from Grandma's horrified face.

Normally, I'd shout, "Milou! What the heck are you doing!? No Barney for a week!"

But today? I let it ride.

Get her, baby. Get her good.

This is culinary diplomacy.

"Ugh…"

Grandma recoils.

For a moment, I worry she's going to faint. But no—she clutches her stomach and makes a dramatic escape to the bathroom like she's in the first trimester of a regretful pregnancy.

I stay in the kitchen, quietly stirring kelp tea, my shoulders shaking with suppressed laughter.

"Milou,"

I say sweetly,

"we're having *tororo gohan* tomorrow."

"Yaaay! Mommy, I love gooey, slimy stuff!"

That's right.

My daughter has beautiful Japanese blood running through her veins.

Take notes, woman.

This is what heritage looks like.

And don't think your day ends with a few sticky soybeans.

Tonight, in honor of our distinguished guests from the California Headquarters, we're going all out.

We're taking you to sushi.

Real sushi.

Seattle's got some of the best sushi joints in America. My dear mother-in-law has always scoffed at our raw fish tendencies—"You people eat fish raw? That's just savage."

Tonight, she's going to stare that sea creature in the eye and smile.

I booked the counter.

Yes, the counter. The sushi counter isn't just seating—it's sacred ground.

It's where the chef becomes your therapist, your food stylist, and your silent *sensei*. It's a tasting menu of trust. A culinary confession booth. You sit. You surrender.

So buckle up, woman. Tonight, the *wasabi*'s real.

John's siblings? Oh, they love sushi. *Toro! Hamachi! Ikura!* Flying left and right.

Meanwhile, my dear mother-in-law?

She's starving. She skipped the sticky breakfast, screamed "SNAKE!" at the *unagi* I lovingly prepared for lunch, and has been running on fumes and spite ever since.

"Please, help yourself."

A daughter-in-law's gentle offer. Almost too kind. The starving woman scans the sushi counter like it's a crime scene.

These… these raw corpses!

She recoils. Then turns to the sushi chef with the grace of a medieval queen and declares:

"I'll have well-done beef, please. With a knife and a fork."

I blink. The sushi chef blinks. A piece of *uni* blinks. But okay. The lady wants beef? Beef she shall get. Overcooked. Brown as her soul.

She pulls poor Colonel Dad—who's happily chomping on a piece of *chu-toro* with his kids—back into her orbit.

"You're eating what I'm eating,"

she commands.

"B-but… I want sushi too…"

Colonel Dad's voice trails off. Now he's sitting next to her, the fork in the left hand, the knife in the right, obediently carving into a sad slab of teriyaki beef.

As he saws through the meat—*geek-geek-geek*—the woman chews, plots, and thinks to herself:

"That daughter-in-law must be stopped."

The Japanese daughter-in-law she reluctantly accepted. But deep down? She still hates it. HATES. IT.

The moment I step out of sight, she snatches John like a sneaky old hawk and whispers:

"International marriages must be so difficult, don't you think?"

Here we go again.

Never mind the years of holidays, forced vacations, and sushi diplomacy. She always circles back to the same tired script:

"Japanese people are barbaric!"

"The child will be a total wackadoodle!"

That child?

Born from my *uncivilized* womb?

Oh, she's not just "acceptable" now. She's been rebranded—a bilingual prodigy!

The same little girl who kisses you with a mouth full of *natto* and answers to a "weird, un-American name" you used to hate?

Yeah. That one. The one you now adore like she's a Disney princess dipped in soy sauce.

Admit it, lady.

Your precious grandchild is carrying on your bloodline —with a heavy pour of Japanese beauty.

She's not a copy of one nation—**she's a masterpiece of international collaboration.**

And let me make one thing crystal clear:

No matter how many years I live in this country—

No matter how much turkey I carve—

My eyes will stay black, my skin will stay yellow, and I will NOT be bleaching my soul for your approval.

I am proud to be Japanese.

I said it once, and I'll say it again.

Years have passed since I snatched your golden boy and married into this family, but has anything changed?

Not a damn thing.

I'm still the odd one out.

But guess what?

I.

Don't.

Lose.

Not to you.

Since the legendary "Christmas in Seattle" showdown, the woman has doubled down on everything—calls, comments, calendar invites.

The question looms:

Will the Seattle Branch hold the throne?

Will the woman reclaim her empire?

Well, she can try.

But I've got John's butt in a motivational headlock and I'm not letting go until we plant the flag of independence right in our own backyard.

Seattle shall rise.

CHAPTER 25

THE VAGINAL ENCORE

**"WAAAAAAAHHHH!
GYAAAAAAAHHH!"**

Whoever said the second one just pops right out—
LIED.

Five years after my first, I was back in the same posh,
spa-like birthing suite—jacuzzi, shower, TV, even a
VCR!—because streaming was still science fiction
back then.

And in the fridge? A bottle of Dom Pérignon with a
label scrawled in fat Sharpie: **MEGUMI'S DO NOT
TOUCH!**

Five years earlier, the Sharpie had marked on beer.
Look at me—moving up life!

Champagne upgrade aside, the soundtrack was the
same. I was making sounds no human should ever
make outside a haunted house, just like five years ago.

This time, though, I'd gone full All-American Good Girl Pregnant mode. No dramatic water-breaking. Just steady weight gain until I became a human meatball with feet.

John? He'd learned.

He stayed wisely parked in the far corner of the room, out of my arm's reach, quietly hyperventilating.

No "hee-hee-hoo" breathing this time. Good boy.

"Damn it! I swore I'd never do this again!"

I had zero intention of recycling John's genes. But then came the soft sell:

> "Only children get lonely…"

> "Wouldn't it be nice to have a son?"

John said that.

Okay, fine—I said that.

Yes, I wanted a son. A soft-spoken mama's boy who'd do whatever I say.

And so, there I was—flailing solo on a hospital bed like a beached whale, dignity long gone, about to deliver another one of John's offspring. Naturally. Again.

I was starving.

I wasn't hooked up to the IV this time, but they still wouldn't feed me until I pushed the baby out.

Why are they so mean?! Seriously. Just give me a rice ball. I'll push harder, I promise.

"GWAAAAHHH! I'M HUNGRY! GIVE ME FOOD OR THE DAMN EPIDURAL!"

"Oh dear… do you think it's still not too late?" the young nurse asked sweetly.

"SHUT UP AND DO IT! BRING THE BIG GUNS!"

"Okie-dokie~"

She skipped off.

Everyone told me, "The second one's easier."

So I figured I'd tough it out naturally again.

But by 10 p.m.—after an all-day labor marathon—I was done.

Five years ago, I believed a mother must endure pain to bond with her child. But now? I'd been in America long enough. Time to Americanize my crotch.

"I brought him for yaaa~!"

The nurse returned, towing in the anesthesiologist like a pizza delivery guy.

He was my hero.

"Sit up on the bed," he said.

"We're going to insert it into your spine, okay?"

"Stick it wherever—just STICK IT!"

I made myself very clear.

"Roger that."

SQUELCH.

   "AIEEEEEE!"

That wasn't me—it was John. The needle was so huge it triggered his fight-or-flight reflex.

As for me? Already in hell. They could've hit me with a tranquilizer dart, and I wouldn't have flinched.

"Alrighty then, your lower half is officially numb-numb~!"

And just like that—bam—I was rescued.

The power of the epidural: divine.

Epidurals forever!

Long live painless childbirth!

Just a minute ago, I was doubled over in pain with every contraction. Now? I was calmly watching the monitor.

"Oops, looks like I'm having a contraction."

"Huh, maybe it's time to push."

I said these things like I was narrating someone else's

birth—like some polite midwife just observing another lady's situation.

Dear God, why didn't I get this epidural earlier?! Why did I get all sentimental about "natural childbirth" again?

I wasted all day flopping around like a beached whale for absolutely no reason. Major regrets.

"You know," the nurse said brightly,

"Next time, you can just start with the epidural."

"THERE IS NO NEXT TIME, YOU FOOL!

I'm never birthing another one of his kids again!

Can you just snip his penis now?"

"That hurts!"

John squeaked.

"All right, it's go time!" the nurse beamed.

"Oh, we're at max contraction already? Okay then!"

With legs like overcooked *udon* noodles, I gave a few limp pushes.

   "Waaaah!"

From between my floppy legs, a baby's cry.

I had officially squished out a human being.

And I stayed cool, calm, and shockingly collected to the very end—like a total pro.

Hope you're impressed, kid.

Well, so much for the classic Japanese line,

> "You're precious because I suffered to give birth to you."

Guess I'll go with,

> "I went through half of hell to bring you here!"

Wait—this is no time for jokes!

"Is there a penis?"

I shouted.

"I don't see one,"

John replied.

> "WHAT DO YOU MEAN YOU DON'T SEE ONE? FIND IT!"

They searched the baby.

The bed. The floor.

No sign of a tiny little anything dangling anywhere.

—Nothing.

"It's another girl," the nurse said, with an apologetic smile.

I turned to John.

"Guess your sperm didn't have what it takes."

And just like that, another fearless female joined our warrior clan.

Oh god.

Here we go again.

—Breastfeeding. Poop. Pee. Repeat.

Twice now.

I've opened the gates.

NEVER AGAIN.

From this moment on, these legs are on permanent lockdown.

CHAPTER 26
MILAY THE WACKADOODLE #2

We named the second baby Milay—a perfect match for Milou's little sister.

See, in Japanese, "Milou" becomes "Miru."

The conjugation goes: miru, mire, miro.

If you know, you know.

I wanted their names to follow that same grammatical rhythm—just like the old Japanese anime *Humanoid Monster Bem* (妖怪人間ベム).

If you know that, you're a true anime *otaku*!

The main characters—three monsters dreaming of becoming human—were Bem, Bera, and Bero.

Bem, Bera, Bero.

Miru, Mire, Miro.

Poetic, right?

So the second one had to be *Mire*. We spelled it Milay.

And the third, Miro?

No more. Maybe in my next life.

Anyhow, here's the real genius behind the name Milay:

All of Milou's stuff? Labeled head-to-toe with a permanent marker—"Milou." And I wasn't about to let all that go to waste. So what did I do?

Gave the "o" a cute little tail—boom, it's an "a."

Slapped a line through the "u"—hello, "y."

Magic trick complete: Milou → Milay.

Milay would happily inherit Milou's hand-me-downs, unaware that her onesies had lived a past life.

Eco-friendly, budget-friendly, stylishly deceptive… and sneakily brilliant.

Naming her Milay? That was peak ex-copywriter brilliance, thank you very much.

I patted myself on the back, about to celebrate with another bottle of beer—

And then… it hit.

A storm.

Straight from California.

"HOLD IT RIGHT THERE WITH THAT NAME!!"

Cue the dramatic entrance—my dear mother-in-law, barreling in through the phone like an angry bull.

Again.

Just like five years ago.

She'd been meddling for months—even before the birth.

Again.

> "Name her Mary!"

> "If not Mary, then Sarah!"

> "No? Then Barbara!"

Relentless.

On a holy mission to slap some long-dead relative's name onto my fresh, innocent newborn.

She'd already *lost* the naming war with our first child. So now? She was back—with a vengeance.

A branding mission.

A legacy of doom.

"Well, it might be a boy," John had mumbled weakly.

Which only made things worse. The moment she heard there was no tiny pee-pee down there? Boom. She pounced.

> "Pick one of MY names—or else!"

Like hell I would.

I'm no rookie.

And this warrior queen? Doesn't bow to ghost-name ultimatums.

—And that's when The Name Nazi activated full beast mode. She started calling. Every. Single. Day. Desperate to cancel Milay before the ink dried.

"It's not even a real American name!"

Deja vu. Didn't we do this exact dance when Milou was born?

Then came the drama:

"Milou and Milay sound too similar! She'll grow up confused and become a total wackadoodle!"

And for the grand finale:

"I've spoken to the California clan. We ALL disapprove!"

Oh, she came fully loaded—firing off every insult in the Name-Shaming Playbook. Determined to erase Milay's existence before it had even begun.

At first, I was willing to compromise. Let her cursed family relic sneak in as a middle name.

But then—

SHE. WENT. TOO. FAR.

Excuse me?!

Not an American name?

And who exactly gets to decide what counts as American?!

Naomi is American.

Hussein is American.

There are Americans in every shade and every spelling!

And your precious John?

That name's officially a dog name in Japan now.

Bow-wow. Woof!

Honestly, the real mistake was telling her anything at all.

Seattle declared independence from California years ago—what was I thinking?! If I don't rise up and take the throne now, when will I?!

I filled out the birth certificate myself:

First name: Milay.

Middle name: Midori

Midori is my late grandmother's name.

Yes, *that* Grandma—who survived the Tokyo fire-bombings by American B-29s, lost everything, and still never hated Americans.

A true humanitarian.

That's the name my daughter will carry.

Sorry, Mother-in-Law.

Your dusty old legacy won't even make it to the middle name slot.

Milay, bearing my grandma's name, will grow up with a heart just like hers—Strong. Gentle. Unshakably kind.

That's the legacy I'm passing on.

But The Name Nazi wasn't done.

She refused to say Milay's name.

Instead, she went with:

> "Baby M."
>
> "Little M."
>
> "Milou's sister."

Anything but the name we chose.

And then... the next bomb arrived in the mail:

A book on gender selection.

Yep.

This woman mailed us a literal manual titled: *How to Make a Boy.*

"YOU'RE THE ELDEST SON'S WIFE! GIVE US A MALE HEIR!"

Wait.

Hold on.

Aren't international babies like ours the supposed downfall of civilization, according to you?

Didn't you say our kids would grow up to be cross-cultural wackadoodles with no identity?

And now you want one of them to carry your bloodline?

Oh, so you *do* like mixed babies—just the penis-equipped kind.

Unbelievable.

Nope.

Not happening.

What are you—secretly Japanese?

Save that heir obsession for your samurai TV reruns.

I.

AM.

DONE.

Milou and Milay.

Your names might sound like a French pop duo—

But they're magical.

Fierce. Distinct. Unmistakably global.

Own them.

Wear them like armor.

They're even cool enough for Monsterland.

That's how cool you are.

Because in this family?

We don't follow rules.

We rewrite them—one name at a time.

CHAPTER 27
LET'S GO FEISTY!

"I've never met a Japanese person like you."

"You're really funny!"

Ever since I moved to Seattle, I've been hearing that kind of thing from Americans.

And I get it. What they're really saying is:

"I never paid much attention to Japanese people before."

"You're surprisingly funny—for a Japanese."

I can smell the condescension behind the compliments.

Their surprise says it all—expectations were low.

Being a foreigner is exhausting.

Living in America, I've been judged for being:

Japanese. Asian. An immigrant.

It happens.

A lot.

At the grocery store, the cashier is all chatty with the white lady in front of me, then dead silent when it's my turn.

I go out for fancy steak with my Japanese friends— horrible service. But the moment John shows up? Instant attitude adjustment.

To the ones who ignore me, I shout,

"HELLO, HOW ARE YOUUUU?"

right in their smug little faces.

When service is blatantly racist, I don't just complain. I write letters to management.

I've collected so many "we're sorry" coupons over the years—from local coffee shops and fancy restaurants to airlines and beyond.

When will I stop doing that?

When people can accept every skin color and every accent that comes with speaking English.

I've been called too loud, too bold, too much.

And now? I wear it like a crown.

To every woman who's been told she's too much:

Good.

Be more.

To every immigrant who's still figuring out:

Same here.

But don't shrink. We're not a burden. We're the spice that brings the whole dish to life. We're not just wanted. We're needed.

To every mama who's doing her damn best in a world that keeps moving the goalposts:

I see you.

You are not alone. You've got a whole tribe willing to support you—you just have to look around and let them in.

"You are so feisty!"

A new acquaintance once told me that at a friend's party.

I wasn't sure if that was a compliment or sarcasm.

I looked at her quizzically.

She smiled and added,

"It is good to be feisty."

That was my first real encounter with the word "feisty" —and I've been in love with it ever since.

I've been described in many ways before, but this one? It was a revelation.

I thought, *I am feisty. And I'm proud of it.*

And I smiled back.

The word "feisty" is often translated with negative terms like "bossy "or "aggressive."

But it also means Spirited. Bold. Full of Energy.

I'm here to redefine "feisty" as a badge of pride.

So I did something about it.

I started **Go Feisty!**—GoFeisty.com.

Go Feisty! was created to support spirited and energetic Japanese women living with courage and confidence.

But today, **GoFeisty!** is for everyone.

It's for anyone striving to live the feisty way of life—a 24/7 lifestyle brand for spirited souls everywhere.

Be Strong. Be You.

That's the message I want to send to anyone who needs the push to begin.

And now, I'm building a global FEISTY community—

One story, one voice, one fearless step at a time.

This wraps up *FEISTY: The Accidental Beginning.*

This book is an original work inspired by a Japanese-language book I published years ago.

It's not just a translation—it's a reinvention to speak directly to English-speaking readers.

This whole ridiculous journey?

Just the first chapter of my immigrant life in Seattle and the wild pre-Seattle years, too.

And yes, it started a few decades (and hairstyles) ago.

Why now?

Well, first of all, it took me forever to sit down and write in English—because I was too busy being a mama to two feisty daughters.

I also spent years trying different gigs, figuring out what my true calling was.

—And maybe the timing had to be just right.

The storms from California finally stopped blowing my way.

And now I know:

I want to be a storyteller for the rest of my life—on my terms, in my own voice.

I never thought I'd write this in English.

But with everything happening around the word "*immigrant*" lately, I felt the need to speak up—to show what one immigrant's life actually looks like.

Am I getting older?

Hell, yes.

But so what?

I still drink like I did in college.

I still act like a rebellious teenager.

My burp is still a masterpiece.

Defy age.

60 is the new 30!

…Or maybe 40?

Whatever.

If I were a supermodel, I'd probably be jobless and drunk by now.

But lucky me—I'm not a supermodel.

Not a figure skater either.

I don't need youth to prove my worth—or my talent.

My peers back in Tokyo?

They're starting to retire.

Me?

I'm just getting started.

I've aged well—

which only makes me a sharper storyteller.

And I've got so much more to say.

My career peak?

Still ahead.

Thank you so much for reading.

You may have noticed—this book doesn't wrap up with a neat, feel-good ending.

That's because I'm still in it.

Still fighting. Still stumbling. Still growing. Still figuring things out.

But if this book made you laugh—

and sparked even the tiniest fire inside you—

then I'm so glad I wrote it.

To be continued…

Let's Go Feisty!

With Big Love,

Megumi Bear

(Yep—that's my new pen name!)

YEAR OF THE FIRE HORSE

🔥**Blaze in Orange!** 🔥
The Fire Horse—*Hinoe-Uma—returns* in 2026
Only once every 60 years!

LET'S CELEBRATE!

Among the twelve zodiac signs, the Fire Horse is so powerful, it appears only once every six decades. For centuries, Japanese women born under it were branded with cruel superstitions: too strong, too wild, too much.

Well, guess what? *Too much* is now our brand.

Now's the time to rewrite history.

Let the world know: Fire Horse women don't bring misfortune—we bring fire.

Let's flip fear into fireworks in 2026!

Orange is our fire, our symbol of boldness—so let's blaze in orange and celebrate around the world!

🔥For those of us Fire Horses born in 1966—let's celebrate our *kanreki* (還暦, the 60th-birthday milestone) not in traditional red, but in blazing orange.

233

For the brand-new Fire Horse babies arriving in 2026: let's shower them with orange gifts, fierce love, and the kind of global pride no superstition can touch.

For everyone else—it's party time! Wear orange. Gift orange. Blaze in orange all year long in 2026!

Let's make 2026 one giant celebration in orange.

Join the FEISTY2026 global movement, where orange stands for strength, spirit, and fire.

Learn more about FEISTY2026—https://gofeisty. com/trendings/2026proclamation/

Let's raise our voices.

Let's Go Feisty!

www.gofeisty.com